*Thomas W. Guthrie*

# Birth Basics When Jesus was Born

3rd Edition

**Thomas W. Guthrie**

# Birth Basics
# When Jesus was born

## 3rd Edition


ISBN: 979-8-9988546-1-3
Published by Thomas W. Guthrie
Land O' Lakes, Florida 34638

# Dedicated to Dad and Mom:

I didn't invent it but, I have found that, *"the water of the Word is the fuel that powers the engine of life."*

# Acknowledgments

I would like to thank the following people for their advice and suggestions:

Henry Roberts; Frank Oliveto; Ann Marie Oliveto;
Doloras Perrone; Ron Farrugia; Dawn Farrugia;
Pastor Curtis Bradford; Dan Coflin, Phd.

Also, a **special** thanks to Ron Farruiga for taking time to create original artwork for this book.

# Preface

The desire to write this book came about after my interest in the visit to Jesus by the wise men was heightened by a recent teaching during a Sunday school class. The event of the wise men visiting Jesus is recorded in the Bible in the book of Matthew. I have been taught that the wise men could have and probably did visit Jesus about two years after his birth. This perspective was recently reiterated, at which time the question arose in my heart and mind as to why astronomers or astrologers would not hastily search out a king whose star they would have been charting and following for some time. As I began pondering those questions, other questions arose in my mind. I began to wonder about Mary's, Joseph's and Jesus' travels to Egypt. Questions about what things were happening historically during the time when Jesus was born and a multitude of other questions. These questions led to the ultimate question when was Jesus born? This book compiles information from a variety of sources and addresses issued associated with Jesus' birth; Herod, Quirinius Bethlehem, the flight to Egypt. These issues and others are discussed all within the framework of history. You may not be a history buff or a person who enjoys reading factual information but, have *you* ever wondered when Jesus was really born?

# Table of Contents

## Chapter 1

# Questions to Consider

Why would the wise men visit Jesus two years after his birth and not sometime during the first days after his birth? The logic would be of course that they had been charting particular heavenly events, however time would be required to determine the meaning of the events. After determining the significance of the events, time would also be required to travel to the appropriate locale. Hence, a time of two years before the wise men would visit with Jesus.

This logical approach would support the perspective that the wise men from the East would have visited Jesus two years after his birth. One point most always added to support this teaching is the biblical statement in Matthew chapter two, verse eleven, that the wise men, *"...going into the house they saw the child with Mary his mother, and they fell down and worshiped him."*[1] The rationale associated with this statement is that Jesus was born in a manger and not in a house. Therefore, he could not have been visited by the wise men at the time of his birth <u>in a house</u>.

This logic seems sound, however it is shallow and some other questions need to be asked. First of all, we need to consider the wise men and the extent of their knowledge. Would these sages through their previous studies and accumulated knowledge

1 *The Old and the New Testaments of The Holy Bible Revised Standard Version* (All Biblical references are from this version unless otherwise noted.)

foreseen and anticipated the presence of the star? Could these men have been called by God to pay homage to His Son? After all, in Matthew chapter two, verse twelve, the Bible tells us that these men upon visiting Jesus had been warned in a dream not to return to Herod. This dream was undoubtedly from God warning these men and preserving their lives. In the second chapter of Luke, verses eight through twenty, angels heralded the birth of Jesus to the shepherds of the field. Would not also God send someone who understood and recognized His words of prophecy to honor His Son at His birth?

Considering that Mary was just pregnant and not yet ready to deliver her child when she arrived in Bethlehem, she would therefore most likely have been asked to go to someplace available, but not necessarily accommodating - somewhere such as a stable. A stable would provide shelter from the night and a modicum of comfort with the animals and straw. You would think though that once the baby was delivered, no one except the most cruel hearted individual would insist a mother and new born child be kept in a less than desirable environment as a stable. An invitation to repose in someone's house would have probably been accepted by Joseph and Mary. Also, if we consider that the mother and child were visited by hosts of shepherds, knowledge of this child would come to most everyone in the vicinity. With such commotion, would not the innkeeper or someone have acknowledged the presence of this special guest? After considering such questions I believe we need to look deeper at the birth of Jesus.

## Chapter 2

# Chronology

Most studies dealing with Jesus' birth begin by focusing on the star of Bethlehem. Was it myth, or was it a real occurrence? If it was a real occurrence, what was it; a meteor, a planet, a conjunction of planets, a comet, a super nova, or some other astronomical happening not readily explainable? Each scholar has his or her particular "hypothesis" and begins to develop Jesus' birth around the hypothesis in the time frame of the hypothesis. Was his birth related to the conjunction of Jupiter and Saturn in 7 B.C., the comet of 3 B.C., the super nova of 5 B.C. or the comet of 2 B.C.? When considering such hypothesis we must remember that Jesus was a historical figure. As a historical figure, certain historical events surrounding his birth existed and must remain in context of their historical settings. Only then can the events in the heavens be applied to recorded historical events. However, let us turn our attention to the historical events and look at the heavens only as they relate to the reckoning of days, months and years.

Development of a stable calendar, one in which recorded events and festivals would occur the same time each year has been a constant undertaking by different cultures. The establishment of years, one period of a calendar cycle has always fixed upon some specific event. One common way of setting years was to begin the counting of years based on the reign of a new king. This method was usually adequate for the culture that instituted the yearly cycle. However, the understanding of the specific year of an event was limited to the culture that had fixed the cycle and other cultures sometimes would not be able to correlate an event to their cycle of years. Also, as time passed and more and more kings came to power and died, it became burdensome to speak of or write about an event based upon the timing of a particular king's reign.

Another method of determining cycles of years is to set the beginning of the years at a specific event other than the beginning of a king's reign and keep careful accounting of each subsequent year from that event. The Roman Empire established it's cycle of years in this manner, based upon the time the City of Rome was established. Every other event within the existence of the empire was then referenced as a time removed from the establishment of the City of Rome.

The Christian culture also used the method of adopting a specific event as a way to account for a cycle of years. Dionysius Exiguus, a 6th Century, A.D. Christian monk was the first to propose establishing the birth of Jesus as the point of reckoning from which to track the years. The Christian culture adopted this method and event for the reckoning of time. A new way was established to talk about things that happened before a specific event, and things that happened after the event, the birth of Jesus of Nazareth.

The Jewish Culture has used both methods for determining cycle of years. In the forward of the book, *Talmudic and Rabbinical Chronology*, by Edgar Frank, he writes, "The chronological systems used by Jews have undergone many changes in the course of centuries. In the Biblical period the reckoning was from the time of the Exodus; then from the construction of Solomon's Temple, or according to the reigns of various kings. In post-Biblical times the Jews counted by the Selucidan Era, beginning in the autumn of 312 BCE. They continued this system in Oriental countries until the 16th century. Later chronology was according to the destruction of the 2nd Temple; thereafter, the reckoning from the time of Creation was adopted."[2]

When talking about Jesus, an apparent complexity of chronology seems to exist. Jesus is usually discussed from a Christian perspective using the adopted Christian chronology. However, information about Jesus is from sources, which have their perspectives based upon Jewish chronology or have their perspective based upon the Roman Empire chronology.

In order to establish the event of the birth of Jesus as a point to reckon from, the time of another event had to be determined. The most basic fundamental of Jesus' birth is that he was born when Herod, king of Judea was alive. By determining the time of the death of Herod, a point could be established from which to base the birth of Jesus.

As mentioned before, Dionysius Exiguus was the first to propose using Jesus' birth as the event from which to reckon time. Dionysius, when calculating Herod's death using the reckoning of the Roman Empire, calculated Herod's death as occurring in 754 A.U.C. However, he erred in his calculations and Herod's death occurred in 750 A.U.C. Hence, Herod's death actually occurred in 4 B.C. As such, the year of Jesus' birth is established as 4 B.C. instead of a zero starting point, the intended time fixed by Dionysius Exiguus.

Between the time of Jesus' birth and today the world has

---

[2] *Talmudic and Rabbinical Chronology*, Edgar Frank, Forward

adopted many calendars and ways of computing years, leap years, leap centuries, and other various data to keep a stable calendar in which the seasons of the year begin about the same time each year. Although an extended discourse in calendar development and computations is not necessary, it is important that when we reference an event described from different chronological perspectives, whether Roman, Jewish or Christian, that the event is adjusted to the calendar with which we are most familiar. Today, this is the Gregorian calendar. Events must be appropriately placed in the Gregorian calendar so that we can understand them individually and in context with each other.

## Chapter 3

# When and Who

Any study has to have a reference point from which to start. Most of all of the information about Jesus is contained in the Bible. Jesus of Nazareth, the person around who Christianity is established is mentioned very rarely in historic documents or literature of a non-biblical nature. This lack of information though in no way diminishes the fact of Jesus' historicity and even the most skeptical scholar has eventually had to admit that Jesus was a real person.

So, since Jesus was a real person, did live and die in history and relatively little information about him exists outside the Bible, why not use the information contained in the Bible to study his birth? After all, the old testament of the Bible tells of the history, prophecy and customs of the Jews and Jesus was Jewish. More importantly the books of the new testament of the Bible were written with the specific intent to tell about Jesus of Nazareth. The reference point for this study then is the information contained in the Bible. The Bible in 2 Timothy chapter three, verse sixteen, states that, *"All scripture is inspired by God and profitable for teaching, for reproof, for correction and for training in righteousness."* With this reference point in clear focus we will remember that as we address questions pertaining to historical accuracy we must start at our declared reference point and establish it as truth.

The story of the birth of Jesus and events surrounding this story are related to us in the Bible books of Luke and Matthew.

Luke, chapter two gives us a specific insight into the general timeframe when Jesus was born. In verse one of chapter two we read, *"In those days a decree went out from Caesar Augustus that all the world should be enrolled. This was the first enrollment, when Quirinius was governor of Syria."* The second chapter of the book of Matthew gives additional specific information, *"Now when Jesus was born in Bethlehem of Judea in the days of Herod the king..."* Additional information regarding the birth of Jesus in contained in the books of Matthew and Luke and we will draw on this additional information throughout this journey studying the birth of Jesus.

The opening statements in chapter two of Luke and chapter two of Matthew are however, the point at which the journey begins. Two significant times are established in these opening statements. Jesus was born during the reign of Caesar Augustus at a time when Quirinius was governor of Syria and Jesus was born when Herod was the king of Judea.

Four of the people in whom we are interested from this story have already been introduced: Jesus, Caesar Augustus, Quirinius and Herod. There are now six other persons we need to add to the story: Archelaus, Mary, Joseph, Zachariah, Elizabeth and John the Baptist. Introducing all ten of these individuals at this point will help us to visualize how these people and events surrounding each relate to determining when Jesus was born. These ten people are:

- Caesar Augustus was the Emperor of the Roman Empire from 31 B.C. to 14A.D.
- Quirinius was a Roman Consul and Legate of Caesar Augustus from 12 B.C. through 6 A.D.
- Herod was king of Judea from 37 B.C. to 4 B.C.
- Archelaus was the son of Herod. He was the son who was

designated by Herod, in his Will, to reign upon Herod's death. Archelaus ruled Judea as eutharch from 4 B.C. to 6 A.D.

- Joseph was the husband of Mary. Joseph was the stepfather of Jesus.
- Mary was the mother of Jesus and wife of Joseph. Mary was also kinswoman to Elizabeth.
- Zechariah was a Levitical Priest who ministered at the temple in Jerusalem. Zechariah was the husband of Elizabeth and father of John the Baptist.
- Elizabeth was the wife of Zechariah and mother of John the Baptist. Elizabeth was also the kinswoman of Mary, mother of Jesus
- John the Baptist was the son of Zechariah and Elizabeth. He was also a kinsman of Jesus.
- Jesus is

Even though the time of Jesus' birth is based on Herod's death and Herod died in 4 B.C., let us systemically narrow the timeframe for the occurrence of his birth. For confirmation of the general timeframe of Jesus' birth we can refer to the time in which these three people: Caesar Augustus, Herod king of Judea, Quirinius held the titles referenced in Matthew and Luke. Caesar Augustus was Emperor of the Roman Empire from 31 B.C. to 14 A.D. Herod was king of Judea from 37 B.C. to 4 B.C. Quirinius was a Roman Consul in Syria from 12 B.C. through 6 A.D. In order to meet the criteria as set forth in the books of Matthew and Luke, Jesus had to have been born sometime in the period between 12 B.C. and 4 B.C. This timeframe would be the only time when all three individuals; Caesar Augustus, Herod, and Quirinius held the titles as stated in Luke and Matthew.

Luke, in the book of Luke actually tells us the time of year when Jesus was born and the year he was born. He does this in a very detailed and specific manner. He tells us this by utilizing chronologies from a Jewish perspective and from a Roman Empire perspective. In chapter one of the book of Luke we are shown the time of year of Jesus' birth from the Jewish chronological perspective. The book of Luke, chapter two shows us the year of Jesus' birth from the chronological perspective of the Roman Empire.

## Chapter 4

# What About Quirinius

Some of the most, if not the most, difficult questions about the timing of the birth of Jesus comes from the first verse of chapter two of the book of Luke. Luke most vividly and directly states, *"In those days a decree went out from Caesar Augustus that all the world should be enrolled. This was the first enrollment, when Quirinius was governor of Syria. And all went to be enrolled, each to his own city. And Joseph also went up from Galilee, from the city of Nazareth, to Judea to the city of David, which is called Bethlehem, because he was of the house and lineage of David, to be enrolled with Mary his betrothed, who was with child."* The standard interpretative approach to this passage is that: 1) Enrollment has been taken to mean "census" for the purpose of taxation. 2) There is no recorded history of a world census taken during the reign of Augustus. 3) Quirinius was not a governor of Syria prior to Josephus' account of the census of Judea of 6 A.D. After considering these three statements, this passage in Luke is then either made to fit the Jewish historian Josephus" writings or this statement by Luke is considered historically errant. Let us consider Luke's statements in chapter two of the book of Luke.

Luke wrote the gospel of Luke and the book of Acts to a man named Theophilus. It is generally accepted that Theophilus was a wealthy or at least a authoritative gentile from somewhere in Asia Minor. In the books of Acts and Luke references made to date specific occurrence of events are done so using events outside of the region of Judea, essentially from the chronological perspective of the Roman Empire. Luke, in the book of Luke boldly states three events that would allow Theophilus to verify the accuracy of his statement and the timing of it's occurrence: 1) A decree went out from Caesar Augustus that all the world should be enrolled; 2) This was the first enrollment; 3) This enrollment took place when Quirinius was governor of Syria. As mentioned before, these are considered to be errant according to many scholars. The book of Acts is considered to be historically accurate as is the book of Luke, with the exception of verses one through five of chapter two. However, with such accurate verifiable information contained in these two books, why would Luke error in the statement of verses one through five of chapter two? Is there any non-biblical evidence though that would support Luke's statements?

The idea of census first brings to mind the traditional scholarly revered census of 6 A.D., recorded by the Jewish historian, Josephus. The census of 6 A.D. has been adopted by many scholars as being "the census of Luke" as it is a census that somewhat fits the criteria as set forth in the Bible for the time of birth of Jesus. The census of 6 A.D. was conducted in Judea and conducted under the direction of Quirinius. However, these are the only two points of criteria that fit into the time of Jesus' birth.

The census of 6 A.D. was conducted because Archelaus, the eutharch of Judea had been banished and Judea was being annexed to the imperial province of Syria. As a point of fact for those persons willing to substitute the census of 6 A.D. for the census described in Luke, the census of 6 A.D. was not a census of the whole world as Luke describes the census which took place at the time of the birth of Jesus. The census of 6 A.D. was a census conducted exclusively for Judea. Therefore, if you disregard Luke's census you must also disregard the census of 6 A.D. Furthermore, in looking at the entire scope of events, which pinpoint the timing of the birth of Jesus, the census of 6 A.D. does not fit in the possible time span. Herod died in 4 B.C. The census of 6 A.D. was conducted ten years after Herod's death. One key and basic point to remember is that Jesus was born during the reign of king Herod.

Also, throughout the debate about Luke's statement in chapter two verse one of Luke, the academic community has translated the Greek word "apographo" to mean "census", reflecting the idea of a census for the purpose of taxation. Debaters supporting Luke's statement have brought forth historical evidence that persons involved in census' during Roman rule were required to return to the place of "lineage", such as was the case with Joseph returning to Bethlehem because he was of "the house of David'. From *The Legacy of Egypt* edited by S.R.K. Glanville, a cache of papyri recovered from Egypt written at the end of Trajan's reign clearly shows that each head of the household was required to return to their own place during a census.[3] And, as Luke describes in the book of Luke, each head of the household had to bring along all the members of his family. Thus, there is non-biblical evidence of requirements of procedures for conducting a census. Those disagreeing with Luke's statement contend that "the historical evidence" just related is from Egypt and is from a time too far removed from Luke's time to be appropriate (approximately 100 A.D.). Opponents also continue to state there was no decree from Augustus for a world census.

Although there is evidence of census procedures, and the census described in the Egyptian papyri show that the census was conducted for the reason of taxation, we need to look at an element of history regarding taxation during Herod's reign in Judea. Again, the Greek word "apographo" has been translated

---

3 *The Legacy of Egypt*, edited by S.R.K. Glanville, p. 276, 278

and interpreted to mean a census for the purpose of taxation. However, Herod during the early period of his reign over Judea aptly maneuvered himself to an advantageous political position. Herod made special arrangements with Caesar and Cleopatra so that neither he nor his kingdom was required to pay taxes to Rome. Augustus, reigning after Caesar, honored this special arrangement and Herod throughout the rest of his reign did not pay taxes to Rome.[4] As such, any decree of a world census for the purpose of taxation would have included Judea and would have been contradictory to Herod's special arrangement for exclusion from taxation. Therefore this census (enrollment) mentioned by Luke must refer to something other than a taxing census.

Augustus, as emperor of Rome had extensive power to make decrees, "For certain things, the Emperor issued commands valid throughout the Empire...The provinces, therefore, would appear to have supplied regular quotas of men and money, which could not be altered except by special order... Probably in this connection the Emperor was authorized to conduct the general provincial census."[5] Augustus managed manpower, talent and resources exceedingly well. One method for obtaining qualified men for administrative posts was to conduct a census of the Equestrian Order.[6] It also appears apparent that decreeing a census may have filled many civil servant posts.

Luke states that a census was conducted by Quirinius. New archaeological discoveries also have revealed evidence of a census directed by Quirinius. An inscription found in Syria is

---

4 *In the Provinces of the Roman Empire From Caesar to Diocletian*, Theodore Mommsen, p. 190, 191

5 *The Augustan Principate in Theory and Practice during the Julio-Claudian Period*, Mason Hammond, p. 55

6 *The History of Human Society - The Romans 850 B.C.-A.D. 337*, Donald R. Dudley, p. 166

translated as follows:

> "Quintas Aemilius, son of Quintue, Secundus, of the Palestine tribe, I have received decorations in the camp of the deified Augustus under Publuis Selpicius Quirinius, legate of Caesar of Syria, and was prefect of the First Augustan Cohort and the Second Naval Cohort. I also by order of Quirinius held the census of the city of Apamea, 117,000 citizens."[7]

A footnote to this inscription by the editors states that this inscription relates to the census of 6 A.D. recorded by Josephus. However, the census referred to by this inscription is a census of the city of Apamea. Apamea was a city in Syria. The census of 6 A.D. recorded by Josephus was conducted for Judea only. This shows us that Quirinius conducted a census other than the census of 6 A.D. Although the exact reason for the census recorded by Luke may not be currently known, historical documents do shed light on the fact that censuses were conducted for reasons other than just taxation. Now that the question of the census has been addressed - what about Quirinius?

In order to fully understand the importance of Quirinius, you need to understand who he was and where he was geographically located during the time of Jesus' birth. You also need to understand a little about the leadership hierarchy during the reign of Augustus.

Who was Quirinius? The man mentioned by Luke as Quirinius, governor of Syria was Publius Sulpicuis Quirinius –

---

7 *Rome The Augustan Age: A Source Book*, Part 1 edited by Kitty Chisholm and John Ferguson, Part 2 edited by Kitty Chisholm, p. 116

"Publius Sulpicuis Quirinius, after having been consul in 12 B.C. had distinguished himself by leading a successful expedition against the wild Homanadenses in Asia Minor near Galatia..."[8] Quirinius is also described as, "a Roman senator who had proceeded through all the magistracies to the consulship and a man who was extremely distinguished in other aspects."[9] As consul, Quirinius was qualified to be a legate of Augustus. A legate was the personal representative to the emperor in a province controlled exclusively by the emperor, for his benefit. Such a province was called an Imperial province. Quirinius was the legate of the Imperial province of Syria.

Many scholars writing about the birth of Jesus hinge the timeframe of his birth around when Quirinius was governor of Syria. They then establish the date for this governorship at 6 A.D. when Quirinius conducted a census of Judea upon the banishment of its eutharch, Archelaus. However, even a cursory study of Roman history shows that Quirinius was never the governor of Syria. This fact is expounded upon by other scholars, upon which they conclusively declare that Luke's account of a census conducted by Quirinius is not only errant in time, but also errant in fact.

Quirinius was never governor of Syria, however beginning in 12 B.C. he was legate of Syria. At various times he is also described as being the governor of Galatia and other territories in Asia Minor. A close look at Roman provincial history reveals some very interesting and important information about Quirinius and Syria.

---

8 *Josephus: Vol. 9 p. 2; English Translation by Louis H. Feldman.* This is an exposition by the translator as to who Quirinius was.

9 Ibid.

Syria, an Imperial province, was always placed under the control of a legate of consular rank and was the center for military control for the region.[10] More importantly, Roman troops were stationed in Syria and not in Galatia.[11] The documented wars of the Romans against the Homonadenses in which Quirinius' name frequently appears, were conducted by the Syrian army under the control of Syria's legate, Publius Sulpicius Quirinius.[12] In fact, "Under the legate's control was a strong military force of four legions, consisting in the early empire almost entirely of Italian Troops. The legate of Syria was responsible for the security of Roman possessions throughout south-western Asia."[13] Syria at the time of the death of Herod was an Imperial province under the direct control of Augustus through his personal representative, or legate, Quirinius. Although the references to Quirinius by Luke is translated as governor, the understanding and differentiation between legate and governor nay not have been a necessity. The sufficiency to explain to Theophilus that is was Quirinius, the governor to which he was referring and not some other. After all, even scholars of Roman history do not always make the exact distinction of the proper rank. As a footnote regarding the inscription concerning the census of Apamea previously related, the editor writes, "The events mentioned in 11.9-14 took place during the second tenure by Quirinius of the Governorship of Syria in A.D. 6 (the first was in B.C. 3-2)"[14] [emphasis added].

---

[10] *Syria A Short History: Being a Condensation of the Author's 'History of Syria including Lebannon and Palestine'*, Phillip K. Hitti, p. 77

[11] [12]*The Provinces of the Roman Empire from Caesar to Diocletian*; Translated with the Author's Santion and Additions by William P. Dickson, Theodor Mommsen, p. 364

[12] Ibid

[13] *Syria A Short History: Being a Condensation of the Author's 'History of Syria including Lebannon and Palestine'*, Phillip K. Hitti, p. 77

[14] *Rome the Augustan Age; A Source Book*, Part 1 edited by Kitty

Quirinius was in Syria from 12 B.C. till after Herod's death. Regardless of the exact title he had, Quirinius was the leader of the Imperial province of Syria with full power and authority of governor.

When studying history we must always remember that the proverbial "sands of time" cause memories to languish and literally engulf and hide evidence of events. Therefore, any event becomes a puzzle to those who study the event at anytime removed from its occurrence. Generally, the farther removed in time from the event, the more pieces to the puzzle there are. In order to assess an event, we must put the puzzle together. There are times however, when some of the pieces to the puzzle are missing. When a piece is missing we must continue to look for it. We cannot force it into the location. Such is the case with the world census decreed by Augustus when Quirinius was governor (legate) of Syria. The Bible shows us that a specific event (the census) did occur in a specific time (when Quirinius was governor of Syria), but we do not know the specifics of the event (the reason of the census). Lost information however, does not negate the picture of the puzzle itself.

Since we have established that the information about the enrollment and Quirinius as recorded by Luke is accurate, we can explore the question: When was Jesus born? We know that his birth occurred sometime between 12 B.C. and 6 A.D.

---

Chisholm and John Ferguson. Part 2 edited by Kitty Chisholm, p. 116

## Chapter 5

# Days and Years

Just as the appeared complexity that exists surrounding the event from which to reckon time, there is also an appearance of complexity that exists as to when the year begins and its length in days. Of the calendars that exist in today's world, which one do we use? How do we correlate data from different perspectives?

The Gregorian calendar is the calendar used in most of the world today. The year consists of twelve months, begins in the winter season in the Northern hemisphere in the month of January and has 365 days. In order to assure that the seasons begin the same time each year the months have a variable amount of days and every fourth year add an extra day to the month of February.

Of course, the Gregorian calendar is basically a calendar based and developed upon a Christian perspective, however Jesus was Jewish. Shouldn't we then use a calendar used by the Jewish culture? Maybe so, but which one should we use, the civil calendar or the religious calendar?

The Jewish civil calendar and the Jewish religious calendar are similar to the Gregorian calendar in that these calendars adjusted so that the seasons begin the same time each year. However, the Jewish civil calendar and the Jewish religious calendars are also adjusted so that the various Jewish feasts and celebrations occur specifically at the time established in the Bible and by tradition. The mathematical calculations and astronomical observations required to make adjustments are so complex that the calendars can only be established one year in advance. The Jewish civil calendar and the Jewish religious calendar are basically the same and have similar cycles. The civil calendar begins the year in the fall season of the Northern hemisphere, in the month of Tishri around the time of the end of September of the Gregorian calendar. The Jewish religious calendar begins the year in the month of Nisan, which correlates to the spring season in the Northern hemisphere, the latter March - early April months of the Gregorian calendar.

Oh, the complexities of calendars. Is either of the Jewish calendars relevant? Essentially the religious calendar is. However, since the time frame we are interested in can be narrowed to a time span of two years, we can look at the basic calendar from which the Jewish religious calendar is derived.

Understanding the basics of the historical Biblical calendar and computations gives us an accurate fundamental understanding of how events surrounding the time of Jesus' birth are related. Biblical years are based upon a 354-day year, which equates to a complete lunar cycle. The lunar cycle established as twelve periods of new moon to new moon calculations or twelve months. A lunar month consists of twenty-nine and one-half (29-1/2) days. As one-half of a day is impractical to work with, the months alternate between thirty and twenty-nine days. The first month, Nisan contains thirty days and the last month of the year, Adar contains twenty-nine days.[15]

But, wait a minute; doesn't the year consist of 365 days? We know that the Gregorian calendar does contain 365 days and

---

15 *Rabbinical Mathematics and Astronomy*, W. M. Feldman, p. 186, 187

is based upon a solar year. The solar year is established as the time for the earth to proceed from a point in time through two equinoxes. Historians and Biblical scholars have described the Jewish religious calendar and the Jewish civil calendar as a lunar-solar calendar – a combination of the lunar cycles and the solar cycle. In order to match the difference between the solar year of 365-1/4 days and the lunar year of 354 days, a method had to be established which would account for the shift in seasons and yet keep the festivals at their appointed dates, within the appointed seasons. The Jewish Rabbis accomplished this, by intercalating or adjusting the lunar year by adding seven leap months called "Second Adar" within every nineteen years. With this method, the seasons of the solar year and the lunar year would once again coincide.[16]

At this point, let us establish when the year begins according to the Bible. Once we know when the year begins, we can fit events surrounding the birth of Jesus together in a chronological order. According to the Bible, the New Year is established as the month in which the children of Israel came out of Egypt under Moses' leadership. Exodus chapter twelve, verses one and two say, *"The Lord said to Moses and Aaron in the land of Egypt. This month shall be for you the beginning of months; it shall be the first month of the year for you."* The remainder of the chapter explains the keeping of the feast of Passover.

Passover is the major feast observed by the Jewish people. The importance attributed to the Passover cannot be overstated. It is the most important time honored event historically, symbolically and theologically in Judaism. The exact time of its

---

[16] *Becoming a Jew*, Maurice Lamm, p. 307

occurrence is carefully calculated each year and is often used as a reference of time when discussing events associated with Israel and the Jewish people. The time of Passover is clearly defined in Deuteronomy chapter sixteen, verse one, *"Observe the month of Abib and keep the Passover to the Lord your God; for in the month of Abib the Lord your God brought you out of Egypt by night."* We must note that during the course of history, the Jewish priesthood adopted Babylonian names for the months. The cycle of months and festivals remained the same but the names of the months changed. The month of Abib became known as the month of Nisan. The time of the feast of Passover is then at various points in the Bible established as beginning on the fourteenth day of the month of Abib (Nisan). Therefore, Passover is celebrated fourteen days after the beginning of the New Year.

Specifically, the New Year begins at six p.m. on the evening prior to the first new moon after the Vernal Equinox as to local time in Jerusalem, Israel. The Vernal Equinox is the time of the year when the Earth is at the mid-point of it's axis tilt, the time when the sun is directly over the equator between winter and summer in the Northern hemisphere. We know this time of year as spring. Occurrence of the Vernal Equinox can be from the twenty-first of March to the twenty-third of March, as to the Gregorian calendar. Passover is therefore always celebrated in the spring, in the latter part of March or the beginning of April of the Gregorian calendar.

The first new moon can occur from the twenty-first day of the Gregorian month to the fifth day of the following Gregorian month. This would establish the beginning of the new year of the Bible (and the Jewish Religious calendar) at the evening prior to the first new moon after the beginning of spring, sometime between the twenty-second day of the Gregorian month of March (the new moon must occur <u>after</u> the Vernal Equinox) and the fourth day of the Gregorian month of April.

Since we have looked at the length of a year and when the year begins according to the Bible, we can now look at two particular events recorded in the Bible related to the birth of Jesus. The conception of John the Baptist and Elizabeth's sixth month of pregnancy collectively add insight into the timing of the birth of Jesus and help to pinpoint the time of year of his birth.

## Chapter 6

# Conception

The initial information needed to determine the conception of John the Baptist is found in Luke, chapter one. Luke chapter one, verse five, says, *"In the days of Herod, king of Judea, there was a priest named Zechariah, of the division of Abijah; and he had a wife of the daughter of Aaron, and her name was Elizabeth."* Luke chapter one, verse eight, says, *"Now while he was serving as priest before God when his division was on duty, according to the custom of the priesthood, it fell to him by lot to enter the temple of the Lord and burn incense. And the whole multitude of the people were praying outside as the hour of incense. And there appeared to him an angel of the Lord standing on the right side of the altar of incense. And Zechariah was troubled when he saw him, and fear fell upon him. But the angel said to him, 'Do not be afraid, Zechariah, for your prayer is heard, and your wife Elizabeth will bear you a son, and you shall call his name John'..."* Luke chapter one, verse twenty-three, *"And when his time of service was ended, he went to his home."* We then read in the first chapter of Luke, verse twenty-four, *"After these days his wife Elizabeth conceived,..."*

From these passages in Luke we find four important items, which lay a foundation for following the time when Elizabeth conceived. These are: 1) Elizabeth's husband, Zechariah, was a priest during the reign of Herod, king of Judea. 2) Zechariah was of the priestly division of Abijah. 3) Zechariah was on duty when it was declared that his wife, Elizabeth would have a son. 4) Elizabeth did not conceive until after Zechariah's service was ended.

To understand this series of events related to the conception of John the Baptist, it is important to understand the significance of the priestly divisions and the appointment of duty of the priest. The Law of Moses and the ordinances contained within the law are of prime importance in studying the birth of Jesus. The Jewish life revolved around these ordinances. In fact, the laws of Moses and abidance to the ordinances are the essence of the Jewish culture.

The Biblical book of First Chronicles, chapter twenty-four, gives the first insight into the divisions of the priests. David, king of Israel, divided the sons of Aaron into twenty-four divisions. The divisions are organized under the heads of their father's houses. These divisions were then selected one by one, by lot. 1 Chronicles chapter twenty-four, verse ten, says, *"..., the eighth to Abijah, ..."* This information tells us that the division of Abijah was the eighth to be selected. Verse nineteen of First Chronicles goes on to explain how the priests are to carry out their duties. The divisions of priests had been selected by lot and now have been told to come into the house of the Lord according to the procedure established for them by Aaron their father. These procedures are illustrated in verses thirty-three and thirty-five of chapter eight of Leviticus. Specifically verse thirty-five says *"At the door of the tent of meeting you shall remain day and night for seven days, performing what the Lord has charged, lest you die; for so I am commanded."* Verse thirty-three talks about the ordination process of the priest and verse thirty-five tells us of the perpetual ministering duties and the time frame for the ministering duties. Through these verses we know that the priests were required to perform their duties ministering to the Lord for seven consecutive days and nights. This cycle of service is confirmed by the twelfth century Jewish scholar, Maimonides,

"…3. Moses our teacher divided the priest into eight divisions, four from (the house of) Eleazer and four from (the house of) Ithaman. They remained that way until the days of Samuel the Prophet, who, together with King David, divided them into twenty-four divisions. Over each division a chief was appointed. One division a week would go up to Jerusalem to minister. The divisions would change every Sabbath day, one leaving and another entering after it. When all the divisions had completed their service, they would return to the beginning of the cycle."[17] This procedure is the same as is described by Luke in his narrative of Zechariah.

The question now is; at what point in time was this procedure originally initiated? In Exodus chapter thirty verses eighteen through twenty-one, we are told the duties of the priests of the tabernacle and are told that the priestly duties shall, *"'…be a statute forever to them, even to him and to his descendants throughout their generations.'"* Verse one of the fortieth chapter of Exodus shows us when the tabernacle was erected: *"The Lord said to Moses, 'On the first day of the first month you shall erect the tabernacle of the tent of meeting…'"* The verses following this introduction tell of the erection of the tabernacle and the beginning of the service of ministry in the tent of meeting by Aaron and his sons. We have now found out that the cycle of priestly duties were begun when the tabernacle of the tent of meeting was erected on the FIRST DAY of the FIRST MONTH and was to be perpetual from generation to generation. This time frame of the beginning of the cycle of priestly service is confirmed by David during his reign. This cycle is also re-affirmed by Maimonides as noted earlier.

---

[17] *The Code of Maimonides; Book Eight The Book of Temple Service,* translated from the Hebrew by Mendell Levittes, p. 54

So, Zechariah belonged to the division of Abijah, the eighth division of twenty-four divisions; each division ministered at the temple for one week and then ministering duties rotated to the next division; the cycle began on the first day of the first month. This cycle of rotation would therefore have the division of Abijah ministering the eighth week of the year and the thirty-second week of the year. This means that there were only two times that the promise of a son could have come to Zechariah. The first time of the promise would have been at the beginning of the third month, Sivan (the end of April/ beginning of May); the second time of the promise would have been at the beginning of the ninth month, Chislev (beginning of November).

Since the Bible states that Elizabeth conceived shortly after Zechariah's return from ministering duties, let's use the week his service ended and he returned home as the time when conception occurred for Elizabeth. From this information we can then determine that the beginning of Elizabeth's sixth month of pregnancy, the twenty-fourth week (6 months x 4 weeks) was either the thirty-third week of the year (the end of November/ beginning of December) or the ninth week of the year (the end of May/ beginning of June).

This sixth month of Elizabeth's pregnancy then allows us to look at the conception of Jesus and Mary's pregnancy. For the Bible states in the book of Luke, chapter one, verse twenty-six, *"In the sixth month the angel Gabriel was sent from God to a city of Galilee named Nazareth, to a virgin betrothed to a man whose name was Joseph, of the house of David; ant the virgin's name was Mary."* A cursory reading of this verse would make you think that the "sixth month" was the sixth month of the year. However, contextually the passages are related to the story of Elizabeth. The story continues and the angel Gabriel tells Mary that she is chosen of God to bear a son, saying, *"you shall call his name Jesus."*

Gabriel continues instructing Mary in the event that is to take place and in verse thirty-six confirms and qualifies the sixth month, *"And behold, your kinswoman Elizabeth in her old age has also conceived a son; and this is the sixth month with her who was called barren."*

The Bible shows that after the angel Gabriel had visited Mary, she went <u>in</u> <u>haste</u> to visit Elizabeth. Verse thirty-nine of chapter one, in the book of Luke says, *"In those days Mary arose and went with haste into the hill country, to a city of Judah, and she entered the house of Zechariah and greeted Elizabeth. And when Elizabeth heard the greeting of Mary, the babe leaped in her womb; and Elizabeth was filled with the Holy Spirit and she exclaimed with a loud cry, 'Blessed are you among women, and blessed is the fruit of your womb! And why is this granted me, that the mother of my Lord should come to me?...'"* This passage tells us that at the time of Mary's visit to Elizabeth, she (Mary) had already conceived. A close look again at verse thirty-six also enlightens us to the time when Mary conceived. You should notice that in verse thirty-six of chapter one, Gabriel, when talking to Mary, says, *"...Elizabeth in her old age has <u>also</u> conceived a son."* This statement shows that even at this time Mary had conceived.

Now, since Mary had conceived just prior to her visit to Elizabeth, we can roughly determine the time of year when Jesus could have been born. Consider first that normal human gestation if from thirty-eight weeks to forty-two weeks long. If Elizabeth's sixth month was around the end of November and this was just after Mary had conceived, then Jesus would have been born around the end of August. If Elizabeth's sixth month were around the end of May, then Jesus would have been born about the end of February. The following event line shows the timing of the events. For purposes of equating a general time frame of events, the twenty-third of March has been established as a point to begin the New Year. Because the Jewish Religious New Year would begin after the twenty-first of March, this date is accurate enough to show the timing of events of: 1) Zechariah's times of service. 2) The time Elizabeth conceived. 3) The time of Elizabeth's sixth month and the time Mary conceived. 4) The time Jesus could have been born.

(SEE GRAPHIC ON FOLLOWING PAGE)

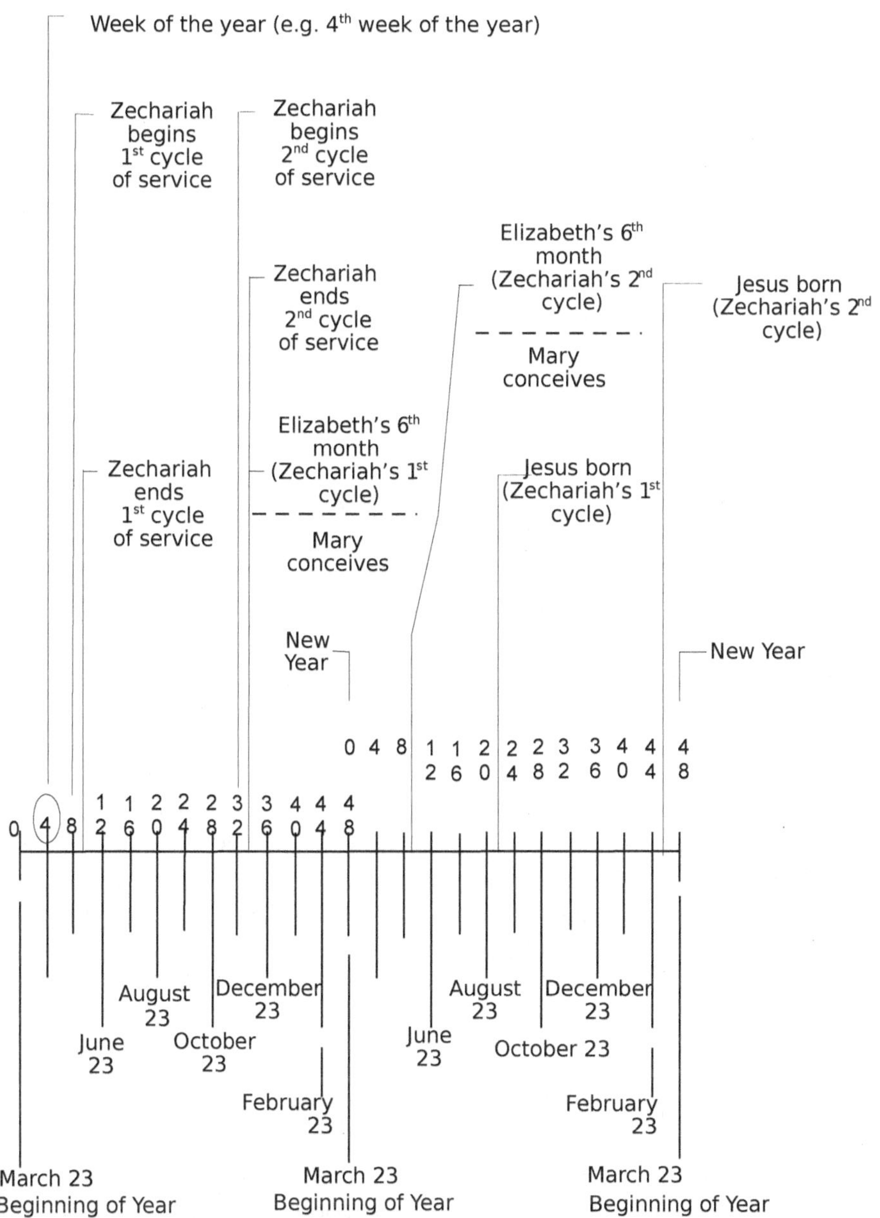
Week of the year (e.g. 4th week of the year)
Zechariah begins 1st cycle of service
Zechariah begins 2nd cycle of service
Elizabeth's 6th month (Zechariah's 2nd cycle)
Mary conceives
Zechariah ends 2nd cycle of service
Jesus born (Zechariah's 2nd cycle)
Elizabeth's 6th month (Zechariah's 1st cycle)
Mary conceives
Zechariah ends 1st cycle of service
Jesus born (Zechariah's 1st cycle)
New Year
New Year
0 4 8 12 16 20 24 28 32 36 40 44 48
0 4 8 12 16 20 24 28 32 36 40 44 48
August 23
December 23
June 23
October 23
February 23
August 23
December 23
June 23
October 23
February 23
March 23 Beginning of Year
March 23 Beginning of Year
March 23 Beginning of Year

To recap:

a. Zechariah was of the priestly division of Abijah. This priestly division began ministering the eighth week of the year and the thirty-second week of the year.
b. Mary conceived at Elizabeth's sixth month of pregnancy.
c. Jesus was born from thirty-eight weeks to forty-two weeks after conception.

Although the priestly divisions are distinctly divided into twenty-four divisions, each division serving twice during the year, you may look at the preceding chart and say, "How can 365-1/4 days, a solar year, consist of forty-eight (48) weeks?" Just as seven months are intercalated during a nineteen-year cycle of the lunar calendar to fix festivals to the same season according to the solar calendar, adjustments were made to the time of service for each priestly division. The exact method for intercalating is undoubtedly extremely complex. However, we can look at the basics from a practical standpoint.

By determining the length of a solar year in the base time of seconds, and subtracting the number of seconds in a synodic lunar year (the time through twelve new moon to new moon observations) we can obtain the amount of difference, in seconds, of these two periods of time.

The calculation:

- Solar year = 365 days, 5 hours, 55 minutes, 25 and 25/57 seconds = 31,557,325.438 seconds per year.
- Synodic Lunar month = 29 days, 12 hours, 44 minutes, 3 seconds = 2,551,443 seconds/month x 12 month/year = 30,617,316 seconds per year

- 31,557,325.438 seconds (solar year) – 30,617,316 seconds (synodic lunar year) = 940,009.438 seconds per year

Dividing this result by twelve gives us the number of seconds per month between a solar year and a lunar year.

- 940,009.438 seconds per year / 12 months per year = 78,334.119 seconds per month.

Then dividing this result by twenty-nine and one-half (29-1/2) days results in the difference, in seconds, during a day between the solar year and the synodic lunar year.

- 78,334.119 seconds per month / 29.5 days per month = 2,655.393 seconds per day

2655.39 seconds per day difference. Let us break these seconds down so that we can better deal with the time involved. One hour is sixty seconds multiplied by sixty minutes (60 x 60), which equals 3,600 seconds (60 seconds per minute x 60 minutes per hour = 3,600 seconds per hour). The difference of time between a solar year and a lunar year is less than on hour a day. To calculate further, we find that the time is:

- 265.393 seconds / 3600 seconds = .737 hours: which equals 44.22 minutes or 44 minutes and 13 seconds per day.

By adding forty-four minutes and thirteen seconds per day to the time a priest worked, the priestly divisions could maintain twenty-four divisions ministering for seven days a cycle and each division serving for two cycles during the year. This would accomplish the cycles of service while maintaining that each division would serve during the same time each year without shifting the time of year that service was rendered.

This idea of working more time during a day may seem absurd. But, time is a relative concept. Just as the time of a year can be calculated on the basis of solar observations or lunar observations, work during a period of time can be adjusted to the practical requirements of the job. From a modern perspective, we actually utilize this method of working more time during the relative time shift when changing from standard time to daylight saving time. During this change from standard time to daylight savings time, anyone working during the time when the change is scheduled to occur (2 a.m.) works on hour longer than is normally worked. Therefore, be assured that the cycles of service for the priestly divisions were adequately calculated to maintain the precise requirements for service. The narrative by Luke about the priestly divisions is accurate to show us the time of year when Jesus was born and Jesus was born either at the end of August or the end of February. How do we determine which time is correct? We must now look at other recorded events in order to determine which time is correct.[18]

---

[18] There is substantial ancient historical documentation that most of the world cultures at one time utilized a 354-day year. Professor Emeritus, Immanuel Velikovsky documents the change of calendar usage from 354 days to 365-1/4 in his book, *World in Collision.*

## Chapter 7

# Herod Alive – Herod Dead

The birth of Jesus and the death of Herod the Great are intricately intertwined. Both events are historically important. Historical events, which occurred during the last days before Herod's death and days immediately following his death each, become singularly important when considering the possible time frame of Jesus' birth. The most detailed recordings of the events in the life and death of Herod are recorded by the Jewish Historian Josephus. It is through study of Josephus' writings of the history of the Jews in Jewish Antiquities and Belle Judaica that great debates as to whether the birth of Jesus really happened and, if so the time of the birth of Jesus. Detailed events concerning the birth of Jesus are found in the books of Matthew and Luke in the new testament of the Bible. These books of the Bible show where and when Jesus was born. The Bible and the works of Josephus, both reliable sources, are usually studied independently of one another. Whenever a comparative study is done of relative portions between the two, polarization occurs. The emphasis then is placed on the events that don't correlate, i.e. the census during the governorship of Quirinius. When this polarization exists, the perspective taken most often is that the works of Josephus are right, true, correct and absolute, and the Bible is deemed errant, inaccurate, and untrue. The historical accuracy of the Bible is then either denounced entirely or is made to fit the information contained in Josephus' works with "apologies", "maybe" and "word studies." In fact many Bible commentators footnote Luke's narrative about Quirinius, citing the census referred to by Josephus and cast dispersions of doubt on the accuracy of Luke's statements. The only thing totally agreed on between these two sources it that Herod died. At this point, it is necessary to refocus and remember that the Bibles has been established as the document of inerrancy and not the works of Josephus. Any seeming historical opposition between the Bible and the works of Josephus must then be mediated with other historical documents. Ironically though, the works of Josephus detailing the events of Herod's death actually support, enhance and clarify the timing of events surrounding Jesus' birth, as recorded in the Bible.

In order to place the timing of Jesus' birth accurately, the events preceding Herod's death and events immediately following Herod's death need to be detailed and approached from a chronological standpoint. Since the works of Josephus are widely accepted by scholars as being reliable in content, we will use his works related to Herod's death and subsequent events to pinpoint the time of Jesus' birth.

The latter days of Herod the Great's life begin in Jerusalem and end with his death at Jericho. Tracing the last days begins from a point in time when Herod was in Jerusalem and a crowd, upon hearing that Herod was dead began to tear down a golden eagle that Herod had erected at the entrance to the temple. Herod though was not dead and had the leaders of the rebellion taken to Jericho and there put in prison. Herod then went to Jericho himself. He then went to the warm springs of Callirhoe on the banks of the Dead Sea and subsequently returned to Jericho. Upon returning to Jericho he had the ringleaders burned at the stake at night. After putting the rebels to death, Herod died. The time of Herod's death is ascribed to the eleventh of Adar, 4 B.C.[19]

---

[19] *Josephus with an English Translation*, Ralph Marcus, Phd, p. 449

Prior to his impending death, Herod revised his Will and appointed heirship and kingship to his son Archelaus. Upon becoming king and announcing his kingship in Jericho, Archelaus did three things in a relative short period of time which allows us to confirm the time of Herod's death and also to view Archelaus' geographical location during this period of time, 1) from Jericho, after declaring himself as king of Judea, Archelaus, traveled with the funeral march to Herodium to bury his father. 2) After burying Herod, Archelaus traveled to Jerusalem. In Jerusalem he went to the temple on Passover and announced his kingship to the crowds gathered for the annual sacrifices. While listening to Archelaus' speech, the crowds became agitated and Archelaus, in his concern for his authority, subdued the crowd and three thousand Passover worshipers were killed. 3) Archelaus, within a few short days after massacring the worshipers on Passover, sailed to Rome for an audience with Augustus Caesar.

From this information we know that Herod was alive on the eleventh of Adar and had died by the time of Passover, on the fourteenth of Nisan. Archelaus became king after the eleventh of Adar, was in Jerusalem on Passover then sailed to Rome a few days later. At the time of the feast of Pentecost, fifty days after Passover, Archelaus was not in Judea.

A span of thirty-two days exists between the eleventh of Adar and Passover on the fourteenth of Nisan. Josephus in Belle Judaica and in Antiquities enlightens us to the things that happened regarding Herod in these thirty-two days between the eleventh of Adar and the fourteenth of Nisan. In Bella Judaica, Josephus tells that the funeral procession for Herod traveled eight stades (one mile) each day in the procession from Jericho, where Herod died, to Herodium, a distance of two hundred stades from Jericho. The time for this funeral procession was twenty-five days. In Antiquities, Josephus tells us that Archelaus, continued to mourn the customary seven days after his father's burial, then on Passover went up to the temple. At Passover Herod had been dead for twenty-five (25) days + seven (7) days or a total of thirty-two (32) days. Thirty-two days! The same amount of days as from the eleventh of Adar when Herod had the instigators of the rebellion in Jerusalem burned at the stake in Jericho, to the fourteenth of Nisan, which was Passover.

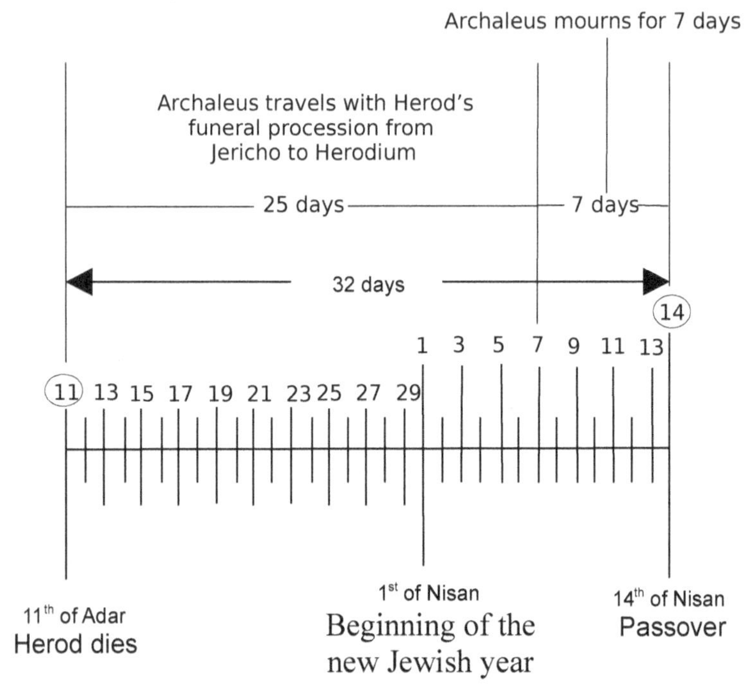

The time of Herod's death is the singular most definitive event related to the birth of Jesus. For we know that Jesus was born when Herod was alive. Although, following the events that happened after Herod's death in order to back track and determine the time of his death are revealing and accurate, a very wonderful, interesting and exciting event happened that allows us to see exactly when Herod died. An event that has been wonderfully recorded by Josephus and confirmed by astronomical calculations, on the night Herod died there was an eclipse of the moon. [20] This eclipse occurred on the eleventh of Adar, 4 B.C.

Another fascinating piece of information provided by Josephus reveals that the night of the eclipse occurred on the night of the fast of Esther. This reason for this fascination is threefold. The fact that the eclipse occurred on a Jewish celebration allows us to see the day of the month and the day of the week Herod died. Also, by giving a specific date of the occurrence of the eclipse, the eleventh of Adar, we have a direct correlation between the date according to the Jewish calendar and the date according to the Gregorian calendar. The eleventh of Adar is the same day as the thirteenth of March. This is indeed an amazing piece of information! The specifics relating to the day of the week Herod died will be discussed later. Right now we will focus our attention on the day of the month and the year Herod died.

To recap; Herod left Jerusalem, went to Jericho then to Callirhoe, back to Jericho, died and never returned to Jerusalem. Herod died on the eleventh of Adar 4 B.C. Because Jesus was born before Herod died, Jesus was born before the eleventh of Adar 4 B.C.

---

[20] *Josephus with an English Translation*, Ralph Marcus, Phd, p. 449

# Chapter 8

# The Law

The mention of the wise men in the Bible is limited, however the visit by the wise men to Herod helps us to finitely determine the time of the birth of Jesus. In order to understand why the wise men were in Bethlehem at the time of the birth of Jesus and why this visit could not have happened at a significantly later date than his birth, we must focus again to Jesus. The Bible shows us in many different ways the places and related events surrounding the birth of Jesus. Historical accounts add to these Biblical accounts by supplying information concerning the time frames involved in these events.

Herod was in Jericho, by the eleventh of Adar, 4 B.C. and did not return to Jerusalem. Therefore, the wise men of the Bible had to have visited with Herod in Jerusalem prior to the eleventh of Adar; *("Now when Jesus was born in Bethlehem of Judea in the days of Herod the king, behold, wise men from the East came to Jerusalem, saying 'Where is he, who has been born king of the Jews? For we have seen his star in the East, and have come to worship him.' When Herod the king heard this, hew was troubled, and all Jerusalem with him.")*.[21] You may say 'OK' the wise men had to have visited with Herod in Jerusalem prior to the eleventh of Adar, but couldn't it have been anytime before then and couldn't Jesus have been born anytime before then?

---

[21] Matthew 2:1-2

A very important fact to remember when discussing Jesus is that, Jesus was Jewish. All traditions and obligations pertinent to the Jews would also be pertinent to Jesus. As such, Joseph, Mary and Jesus would all be required to fulfill all Mosaic obligations. The Mosaic requirements are of themselves constraining to any Jew. However, if we consider the role of Joseph, Mary and Jesus from a theological perspective, and we must, as without a theological perspective the time of the birth of Jesus is a moot matter; then the significance of Mosaic obligations is magnified.

The birth of Jesus or the birth of any male Jewish child of this period in history involved the initiation of three specific rites - the rites of circumcision, redemption of the firstborn, and purifying of the woman after the birth of a child. All three rites involve specific requirements to be completed within specific time frames. These separate events therefore become linked when considering the time element surrounding the birth of Jesus. These Levitical prescribed ordinances have to be completed within the prescribed times in order for the righteousness of the individuals, (the mother and the child) to be initiated and maintained. When dealing with the birth of Jesus the solemnest of these ordinances should be viewed with even greater reverence than the birth of any other child. The underlying understanding of the sanctity of Jesus prompts us to be aware that in order to be the sinless man which Jesus was, requires that the Levitical ordinances be completed exactly as prescribed and within the time frames prescribed by the Levitical law.

The time requirements for circumcision and the woman's purification are addressed in Leviticus chapter twelve, verses one through four; *"The Lord said to Moses, 'Say to the people of Israel, If a woman conceives, and bears a male child, then she shall be unclean seven days; as at the time of her menstruation, she shall be unclean. And on the eighth day the flesh of his foreskin shall be circumcised. Then she shall continue for thirty-three days in the blood of her purifying; she shall not touch any hollowed thing, nor come into the sanctuary, until the days of her purifying are completed.'"* The requirements for cleansing after the time of purifying are told in Leviticus chapter twelve, verses six through eight; *"And when the days of her purifying are completed, whether for a son or for a daughter, she shall bring to the priest at the door of the tent of meeting a lamb a year old for a burnt offering and a young pigeon or a turtledove for a sin offering, and he shall offer it for her; then she shall clean from the flow of her blood. This the law for her who bears a child, either male or female. And if she cannot afford a lamb, then she shall take two turtledoves or two young pigeons, one for a burnt offering and the other for a sin offering; and the priest shall make atonement for her, and she shall be clean.'"*

The requirement of the redemption of the firstborn is found in the eighteenth chapter of Numbers. The reference is made in verses fifteen through seventeen, however, in order to understand the contextual arrangement of this ordinance a reading must begin at least at verse eight; *"Then the Lord said to Aaron, 'And behold, I have given you whatever is kept of the offerings made to me, all the consecrated things of the people of Israel; I have given them to you as a portion, and to yours sons as a perpetual due...(v.15.) Everything that opens a womb of all flesh, whether man or beast, which they offer to the Lord, shall be yours; nevertheless the first born of man you shall redeem, and the firstling of unclean beasts you shall redeem. And their redemption price (at a month old you shall redeem them) you shall fix at five shekels in silver, according to the shekel of the sanctuary, which is twenty gerahs.'"*

Thus the time frames for these ordinances are: CIRCUMCISION – eight (8) days after birth; COMPLETION OF THE DAYS OF PURIFICATION – forty days (40) [(7) days + (33) days]; REDEMPTION OF THE FIRSTBORN – thirty days after birth. [22]

From these time frames it must be understood that in order for the Levitical ordinances to have been fulfilled and Jesus to remain perfect under the Law these things had to have taken place in exactness. We are shown that these ordinances did take place and that they did take place within the constraints of the aforementioned times. However, we must also look at the geographical location in which these ordinances had to take place.

Circumcision is a rite which although requires a specific time frame for it's occurrence, does not require a specific location. In the Bible we find that Abraham and Ishmael and all of Abraham's household were circumcised without the availability of priest or sanctuary. Joshua circumcised the people of Israel while encamped at Gibeath-haaraloth, this episode also occurring without priest or sanctuary. In the customs of the Jews there is no prescribed place for which circumcision has to occur. The rite may be and in many cases is performed in the house of the parents. In today's society the rite may even take place in a hospital. The point of interest is that the circumcision must take place on the eighth day. In *A Guide to Jewish Religious Practice* by Isaac Klein, Mr. Klein states that, "The rite of circumcision is cardinal in Judaism."[23] The importance of the eighth day is addressed in the same book by Mr. Klein: "if the eighth day falls

---

22 The day of birth is counted as day one and then thirty days are to pass before redemption is required. Redemption takes place <u>on</u> the thirtieth day <u>after</u> birth.

23 *A Guide to Jewish Religious Practice*, Isaac Klein, P. 425

on a Sabbath or Festival, the circumcision may not be postponed."[24] Another important event that occurs at the rite of circumcision is the giving of the child's name. The male child is not given a name until he has been circumcised and has come into covenant relationship with God as a result of the completion of circumcision. The circumcision of Jesus could have taken place at any one of many locations. It could have taken place in Bethlehem, on the way to Egypt, or even in Egypt. The Bible tells us that Jesus was indeed circumcised, and at the appropriate time. Luke chapter two, verse twenty-one says, *"And at the end of eight days, when he was circumcised, he was called Jesus, the name given by the angel before he was conceived in the womb."*

Looking again at other Levitical requirements that had to be fulfilled concerning the birth of Jesus: Joseph, Mary and Jesus in order to fulfill the rite of redemption of the firstborn had to be in Jerusalem and offer the sacrifice on the thirtieth day after the birth of Jesus. Of the three rites which needed to be performed during the infant days of Jesus; circumcision, redemption of the firstborn, and the purification of Mary, the redemption of the firstborn was the first that had to take place in the Temple in Jerusalem. We know that this indeed did take place as it is recorded in Luke, chapter two, verse twenty-two and twenty-three... *"And when the time came for their purification according to the law of Moses, they brought him up to Jerusalem to present him to the Lord, (as it is written in the law of the Lord, 'Every male that opens the womb shall be called holy to the Lord')"*. We know therefore that Jesus and his family were in Jerusalem for the rite of redemption, on the thirtieth day after being born. When though did redemption of the firstborn take place, before Herod's death of after?

---

[24] *A Guide to Jewish Religious Practice*, Isaac Klein, P. 425

## Chapter 9

# Journey of Redemption

The redemption of the firstborn is an event that essentially defines other events during the first days of Jesus' birth. As the rite of redemption had to take place in Jerusalem on the thirtieth day after Jesus' birth, there exists a span of time that is narrowly defined. This thirty-day span of time is crucial in determining when Jesus could have been born.

Traditionally, the redemption of the firstborn took place before Herod's death. There are two basic ideas of traditional teaching, each separate and divergent from one another, yet each declaring that the redemption of the firstborn took place when Herod was alive.[25]

The first idea of tradition is that: Jesus was born in Bethlehem, went to Jerusalem to complete the redemption of the firstborn and then returned to Bethlehem at which time the wise

---

25 Traditional teachings not only try to show that the redemption of the firstborn took place before Herod's death but that it also took place before the visit of the wise men. To support this, scholars point out that because Mary offered a pair of turtledoves as burnt and sin offerings and not a lamb she was considered poor. As such, since the wise men gave gifts of gold, frankincense and myrrh, the visit of the wise men to Jesus occurred after the time of redemption and purification of Mary. However, we must realize that the gifts of gold, frankincense and myrrh were <u>given to Jesus</u>. According to Jewish tradition, neither Joseph nor Mary could use these gifts. The gold, frankincense and myrrh were not theirs but were Jesus'.

men visited him. To support this view, scholars point to the wise men's visit to "the child" in a house in Bethlehem (Matthew chapter two, verse eleven). Two points are then emphasized, 1) Jesus was born in a manger and not in a house, therefore he was not a baby; 2) A word study is applied to the Greek word translated to "the child". The word study then shows the Greek word indicates a child of an age older than an infant. The line of logic shows: since the wise men visited Jesus in Bethlehem when Herod was alive and "the child" was older than an infant and the redemption of the firstborn had to take place on the thirtieth day after Jesus' birth; then the rite of redemption took place when Herod was alive.

This idea is an interesting one. However, Joseph, Mary and Jesus never returned to Bethlehem after the rite of redemption was fulfilled. The family went to Nazareth. This is shown to us in Luke, chapter two, verse thirty-nine, *"And when they had performed everything according to the law of the Lord, they returned into Galilee, to their own city, Nazareth."*

The second idea of tradition utilizes the information contained in Luke chapter two, verse thirty-nine and develops a scenario of the family going from Bethlehem to Jerusalem to fulfill the rite of redemption, going to Nazareth from Jerusalem, then at sometime returning to Bethlehem, then fleeing to Egypt. This tradition also teaches that the redemption of the firstborn took place when Herod was alive.

This idea is also an interesting one. But, Matthew chapter two, verses thirteen through twenty-three shows us that Joseph, Mary and Jesus went to Nazareth <u>after</u> they returned from Egypt.

Sometime after Jesus was born, he and his mother and

stepfather left Bethlehem and went to Egypt. This journey to Egypt occurred when Herod was alive, as the Bible states in Matthew chapter two, verses thirteen through fifteen, *"Now when they had departed, behold, an angel of the Lord appeared to Joseph in a dream and said, 'Rise, take the child and his mother, and flee to Egypt, and remain there till I tell you; for Herod is about to search for the child, to destroy him.' And he rose and took the child and his mother by night, and departed to Egypt, and remained there until the death of Herod..."* The beginning of verse thirteen, "Now when they..." is in reference to the wise men. This shows us that the wise men therefore were visiting Jesus prior to Herod's death. These verses also tell us that Joseph and his family fled to Egypt before Herod died. Notice also, that Joseph, Mary and Jesus returned from Egypt after Herod died.

Either traditional teaching declaring that the redemption of the firstborn took place when Herod was alive appears errant when compared to the information contained in Matthew chapter two, verses thirteen through twenty-three and Luke chapter two, verse thirty-nine. The errancy of these traditional views are recognized by some scholars and reconciliation to the scriptures is attempted by elaborating that the books of Matthew and Luke were written to two different audiences and therefore expound on Jesus' birth from a different perspective. As such, the references to the journey to Nazareth in Matthew and Luke are not related. However, you should notice that after detailed narratives, rich in information, both Matthew and Luke conclude events related to Jesus' birth with the family's presence in Nazareth.

Various bits and pieces of information in the Bible are contained in various parts of the Bible. For example, in the book of Matthew it is directly stated that Jesus was born during the reign of King Herod and yet we do not find this information in any other book of the Bible. This information though is not discarded, but becomes a puzzle piece of the entire picture and when fitted with other bits of information, a clear picture is established. Joseph's flight to Egypt and the family's return to Nazareth are two other examples of isolated information. Taken by itself, the time of the flight to Egypt and the length of stay in Egypt can be interpreted in a number of ways. Also, the presence of Joseph, Mary and Jesus in Nazareth can be interpreted in a number of ways. However, when fitted with other pieces of information, the Bible clearly shows when Joseph, Mary and Jesus fled to Egypt and that the stay in Egypt was not lengthy. These other bits of information actually show us the journey of Joseph, Mary and Jesus as though we were looking at an itinerary of their journey.

Jesus was born in Bethlehem and raised in Nazareth. This seems readily simple and straightforward, however the element of the time frames is important. When was Jesus born in Bethlehem and when did Jesus and his family move to Nazareth? After all he and his family did flee to Egypt! In order to understand these events and their timing and relationships let us pick up this story from the Bible at the time of the visitations to Joseph and to Mary by the angels of the Lord.

We are told in Matthew chapter twelve, verse twenty that an angel of the Lord appeared to Joseph in a dream and told him, *"...do not fear to take Mary your wife...as he was betrothed to her and had found that she was with child."* In Luke chapter one, verses twenty-six and twenty-seven, *'...the angel Gabriel was sent from God to a city of Galilee named Nazareth, to a virgin betrothed to a man whose name was Joseph, of the house of David; and the virgin's name was Mary."* In Luke chapter two, verse four the Bible tells us, *"And Joseph also went up from Galilee, from the city of Nazareth."* Nazareth was where Joseph was from, Nazareth is where the angel Gabriel visited Mary and

Nazareth is where Joseph and Mary departed from on their journey to Bethlehem. The beginning of the story of the birth of Jesus begins at NAZARETH.

In Bethlehem, Jesus was born. This is the city of the Messiah as prophesied in the book of Micah, chapter five, and verse one. This particular city of Bethlehem is where the wise men of the story in Matthew were sent by the chief priest and scribes during the reign of Herod the Great. And this Bethlehem is where Joseph and Mary traveled to, from Nazareth, to fulfill the decree of Caesar Augustus. BETHLEHEM, therefore, becomes the second point of reference in tracing the birth of Jesus.

From Bethlehem Joseph, Mary and Jesus go into Egypt. The book of Matthew tells us in chapter two, verse thirteen, "... *an angel of the Lord appeared to Joseph in a dream and said, 'Rise, take the child and his mother, and flee to Egypt, and remain there till I tell you.'*" Verses fourteen and fifteen tell us *"And he rose and took the child and his mother by night, and departed to Egypt, and remained there until the death of Herod."* Neither this narrative nor any other tells us directly the exact time Joseph, Mary and Jesus spent in Egypt. However, the point of interest is that the next place of geography in the birth story of Jesus is Egypt.

Let us step aside from following the itinerary of the travels of Joseph, Mary and Jesus for a minute and examine the geographical border of Egypt during the time of Herod the Great's reign. Sometimes when we read about events from the past we visualize them occurring in a geographical political setting as exists currently in our world. When we read that Joseph, Mary and Jesus went to Egypt, we usually view them as traveling across the southern region of Judea and crossing the Suez Canal, a distance of about seventy miles into the current political regions of Egypt. However, just as the Suez Canal did not exist at the time of the birth of Jesus, the political borders of the country of Egypt were different than they are today. As the region of Galilee to the north of Bethlehem was under the jurisdiction of the Romans and not the client kingship of Herod, so was Egypt to the south of Bethlehem. During the time of the birth of Jesus, Egypt was a mere three days journey form Bethlehem.[26]

After the death of Herod, Joseph takes his family from Egypt back to the land of Israel. It seems as though Joseph may have desired to remain in Israel. However, being warned in a dream, moves on. Let's begin in chapter two, verse nineteen of Matthew to see what the Bible says about this event: *"But when Herod died, behold, an angel of the Lord appeared in a dream to Joseph in Egypt, saying 'Rise, take the child and his mother, and go to the land of Israel, for those who sought the child's life are dead.' And he rose and took the child and his mother, and went to the land of Israel. But when he heard that Archelaus reigned over Judea in place of his father Herod, he was afraid to go there, and being warned in a dream he withdrew to the district of Galilee. And he went and dwelt in a city called Nazareth, ..."* Joseph returned to the city from which he had begun his journey.

Joseph began his journey in NAZARETH with Mary, went to BETHLEHEM with Mary, took Mary and Jesus to EGYPT, journeyed with Mary and Jesus to JERUSALEM in Israel and returned to NAZARETH with his family. These locations are the only places Joseph, Mary and Jesus traveled to in the infant days of Jesus. Not are they the only locations of the family's journey, they are sequenced locations. Any interpreted variation of these sequenced locations is Biblically unfounded.

---

[26] *The Star of Bethlehem An Astronomer's Confirmation*, David Hughes, p. 63

Was Herod alive when the redemption of the firstborn was fulfilled? Since the family returned to Nazareth after the completion of the redemption of the firstborn; and Joseph, Mary and Jesus returned to Nazareth only after they returned out of Egypt; and they came out of Egypt after Herod was dead, the answer is clear. The rite of the redemption of the firstborn took place after Herod's death.

Jesus was born at night. Since Herod died at night and had time to issue an order to kill the children of Bethlehem, he would have been aware of Jesus' birth sometime before the night of his death. Because of this fact and because the redemption of the firstborn had to be completed on the thirtieth day after Jesus' birth, the absolute earliest Jesus could have been borne is twenty-nine days previous to the night before Herod's death. Again, Jesus was born when Herod was alive and came out of Egypt after Herod's death. Twenty-nine days before the night previous to Herod's death was the eleventh of Shebat. Therefore, the absolute earliest Jesus could have been born is the eleventh of Shebat. A birth date of the eleventh of Shebat though would require that Joseph, Mary and Jesus would be in Jerusalem for the redemption of the firstborn on the night Herod died. However, this is an impossibility because Jesus and his mother and father did not <u>come out of Egypt until after Herod died</u>. Therefore, Jesus was born between the eleventh of Shebat and the tenth of Adar. Correlating these dates to the Gregorian calendar, Jesus could only have been born from the eleventh of February [27] 4 B.C. to the twelfth of March 4 B.C.

Throughout the second chapter of Matthew an idea of

[27] It is possible that the eleventh of Shebat could be the twelfth of February, if 4 B.C. was a leap year. However, the first of Adar is the third of March whether 4 B.C. was a leap year or not. As such, all dates subsequent to the first of Adar are not affected by a leap year.

haste and urgency surrounds the story of the birth of Jesus; the wise men – "and being warned in a dream…"; Joseph – "And he rose and took the child and his mother by night, and departed to Egypt."; "in a dream…And he rose and took the child and his mother to the land of Israel." Why was this sense of haste recorded and why was it necessary? The idea of haste is, of course, understandable concerning the wise men's departure out of Israel and also to that of Joseph taking his family out of Israel to Egypt because of the impending wrath of Herod. The urgency to return to Israel though doesn't make sense if one is to consider the traditional idea of a lengthy stay in Egypt for Joseph and his family. Only when considering that important obligations had to be met within specific and very limited time frames do the haste and urgency, as recorded in Matthew, make sense.

4 B.C.

Absolute earliest possible date of Jesus' birth based on requirements of Redemption of the Firstborn
Absolute latest possible date of Jesus' birth based on the fact that Jesus was born when Herod was alive
30 days
32 days
11 13 15 17 19 21 23 25 27 29 1 3 5 7 9 11 13 15 17 19 21 23 25 27 29
1 3 5 7 9 11 13
14
11th of Shebat
(11th of February)
11th of Adar
Herod dies
(13th of March)
1st of Nisan
Beginning of the new Jewish year
(1st of April)
14th of Nisan
Passover
(14th of April)

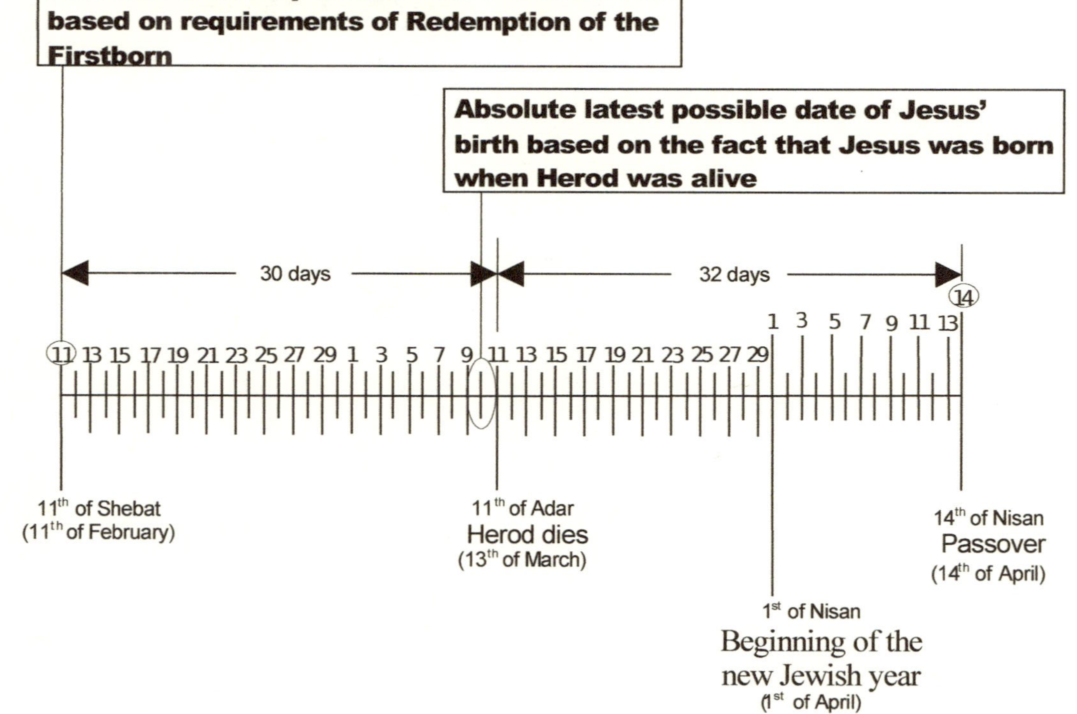

## Chapter 10

# Haste and History

The event surrounding the birth of Jesus as recorded in Matthew indicating a sense of haste confirms that the travels of Joseph, Mary and Jesus from Bethlehem to Egypt, Egypt to Jerusalem, and Jerusalem to Nazareth took place in a very limited amount of time. Why such haste? Remember, certain obligations had to be met in a very short amount of time. Also, historically things were happening in the region. The Bible says that after finding out about the birth of "the king of the Jews" from the wise men, Herod and all the children in the region of Bethlehem two years old and under killed. Josephus tells us of rebellions taking place during Herod's last days of life. Things were indeed happening. Let us now look at what the Bible says was going on in Jerusalem about the time of the birth of Jesus and what Josephus says was going on in the life of Herod.

There exists during the last days of Herod's life a correlation of events between those described in the Bible and events as recorded by Josephus. The Bible, in Matthew chapter two tells us that *"Now when Jesus was born in Bethlehem of Judea in the days of Herod the King, behold wise men from the East came to Jerusalem, saying, (V.1) 'Where is he who has been born king of the Jews? For we have seen his star in the East, and have come to worship him.' (V.2) When Herod the king heard this, he was troubled, and all Jerusalem with him:(V.3) and assembling all the chief priests and scribes of the people, he inquired of them where the Christ was to be born. (V.4)'"* There are five very important points to note from this passage; 1) Jesus was born in the days of Herod the King 2) Wise men came to Jerusalem to worship him who was born King of the Jews 3) Herod, when he heard this, was troubled 4) All Jerusalem was troubled 5) Herod assembled all the chief priests and scribes and inquired of them where the Christ was to be born. It has always been amazing to me that when scenarios are developed to establish the possible date of the birth of Jesus, basics are forgotten. The first and foremost basic point to remember is that, as Matthew state: Jesus was born during the days of Herod. Given to the acknowledged supposition that Herod was a tyrant and adamantly opposed to anyone who might usurp his title and power as king of the Jews, and to the declaration by the wise men and shepherds that a new King of the Jews had been born, shouldn't there be somewhere, some written evidence of this conflict?

This conflict is expressed in the Bible and talks about Herod's command to kill all the children of the age of two and under in Bethlehem. I believe Josephus also discusses this conflict, yet from a different perspective. If we again consider the five important points previously expressed and look at them, not from the perspective of Matthew, but from the perspective of Josephus it is found that the same events are described. It has already been established that the first point is of prime importance and thoroughly agreed that Jesus was born during the life of Herod. Point number two, from Matthew, expressing that the wise men came to Jerusalem to worship him how was born king of the Jews, establishes that the wise men were in Jerusalem. Questions arise as to who were the wise men and from where did they come? These questions have been attempted to be answered by many scholars and authors. Various explanations have been given, from the traditional Christmas theme of three wise men, all the way to an assembly of wise men with an entourage of thousands. Were the men from Babylon, Persia, India? The importance of the men when studying the birth of Jesus relates to not where they were from but how many there were and in what venue of visibility did they arrive in Jerusalem. Questions have always existed in my mind about the presence of the wise men in Jerusalem. How many wise men were there? How did the people of Jerusalem receive them and their inquisitiveness? Was there significant visibility of the wise men as to the entire population of Jerusalem knowing of their presence in the city? How would the population react to questions about a "new" King of the Jews? It would seem that if the population of Jerusalem and Judea felt that Herod was a tyrant, there would be a propensity towards rebellion with such news about a new king.

Matthew records about points three and four that a) Herod was troubled; b) all Jerusalem was troubled. Evidently, the presence of the wise men in Jerusalem was noticed. Their (the wise men's) inquisitiveness and message caught the attention of the populace of Jerusalem and even Herod, so much that everyone became "troubled". Herod, at this point called the wise men to an audience an inquired of their purpose. He then, as point five relates, assembled the chief priest and scribes and inquired of them where the Christ was to be born.

Upon assembling the chief priests and scribes to himself, Herod confirmed two things. He first of all, just by calling the wise men, confirmed that the wise men were on a legitimate mission and their quest was of importance. Secondly, he associated the wise men's inquires - the birth of a 'new' king of the Jews with 'the Christ'. This inference to "the Christ" should not just be seen as a doctrinally inserted phrase by Matthew. After all, the wise men were seeking just a newborn king. Herod, after inquiring of the wise men, came to the conclusion that the king they were in search of was the Christ of the Jews. It was after this conclusion had been made that Herod assembled to himself the chief priest and scribes. Even without the question (where is the Christ to be born?) presented to the assembled learned, the fact he assembled the chief priests indicated the matter was of a religious nature.

At this juncture you say fine and well, but how does this information tie in and correlate with Josephus' writings? Josephus in Book XVII, page 149, writes that when two priests who "were most learned of the Jews and unrivaled interpreters of the ancestral law"[28] upon hearing that the king was dead, instigated a rebellion and preceded to cut down the golden eagle at the entrance to the temple. It is interesting to note that prior to this time there had been no attitude toward open rebellion against Herod from within Judea. Even while living under the ruler ship of a tyrant, the people of Judea lived at this time in a relative secure and peaceable country. Why would two of the most learned priests incite an open revolt? Josephus tells us that the rebellion was started because the two leaders declared that the king was dead. You have to ask yourself, would the king's death be sufficient reason to rebel? Not only to rebel, but to rebel in such an open manner? Also, why would anyone follow these leaders? If the king was dead, why not wait to see how the leadership was going to evolve; one of Herod's heirs ruling, rule from Rome itself? Neither one of these possibilities or a multitude of others would have been agreeable to the Jews, but why an open and seemingly unplanned rebellion?

To answer these questions and others that may not have been asked, but exist in your mind; let us look at Josephus' writings about this event again. We know that two men, Judas and Matthias, were captured and sent to Jericho. Herod followed them to Jericho and had them burned at the stake on the eleventh of

---

[28] *Josephus with an English Translation*, Ralph Marcus, Phd, p. 441

Adar. This is important as it tells that the uprising would have occurred after the visit of the wise men, as Herod never returned to Jerusalem after the eleventh of Adar. Judas and Matthias were, according to Josephus, learned men and men of great religious understanding. Could it be such that these were two of the men called to Herod? Men called to ascertain the place of the birth of the Christ, the newborn King of the Jews? Could it also be that the rebellion took place and had followers because the message was that there was a <u>new</u> king and not that the king (Herod) was dead.

Luke in his account of Jesus' birth, speaks of the shepherds which visited the infant in the manager and *"they made in know the saying which had been told them concerning this child; and all who heard it wondered at what the shepherds told them"* (Luke chapter two, verse seventeen and eighteen). People throughout the countryside had been told of this marvelous birth, but only wondered as to its significance. They may not have understood it, but word had gotten around about this birth. Now, in the city of Jerusalem a great entourage of wise men had come seeking "he who has been born king of the Jews." Surely word about this strange birth had reached the city from the field ad pastures. Judas and Matthias possibly knew the significance of this birth before the visit of the wise men. The talk in Jerusalem about the wise men and their questions would serve to confirm to these two learned men the stories they may have heard coming from the surrounding pasturelands. If indeed, Judas and Matthias had been two of the priests called to audience before Herod with his request about the place of the birth of "the Christ", what an ultimate confirmation of the stories of a fabulous birth. Enough confirmation to begin what Josephus calls an "uprising". The only action recorded as having occurred as a result of the revolt was an assault on the temple in Jerusalem. The specific act of rebellion was to cut down a golden eagle, which Herod had erected over the gate of the entrance to the temple. You must notice that this uprising had sufficient followers to complete the task. Did this action take place in order to cleanse the temple for the Christ? I do believe that, due to the time of the rebellion by Judas and Matthias and the time frame of events surrounding the birth of Jesus, the rebellion was precipitated by the wise men's presence in Jerusalem. The conclusion to this uprising was that the golden eagle above the entrance to the temple was cut down, and the leaders of the uprising, Judas and Matthias, were burned at the stake on the eleventh of Adar. Yet, conflict between seekers of the new king and Herod do exist. Herod had once again squelched any attempt to dissolve him of his kingship.

We have discussed events taking place in Jerusalem just prior to the death of Herod. Now let us look at an event within the first days of Archelaus' reign. An event similar to the events just described. Viewing this event also from two different perspectives.

The time from the death of Herod to Archelaus' journey to Rome is a very short period. Josephus makes it plainly clear that Archelaus left for Rome shortly after his troops had killed 3,000 worshipers during Passover in 4 B.C. By the time of Pentecost, seven weeks later, a major struggle for power was going on in Judea. Saturnius and Varus were determining which of them would bring order to Judea, and the men Archelaus had left to guard his heir ship were struggling to maintain the inherited kingdom.

It has been proposed by some that Archelaus did not leave for Rome in the same year as his father's death, but the year after. It is crucial to understand that Archelaus did go to Rome in 4 B.C. Upon the death of Herod at Jericho, Josephus writes, '...The next thing was that Ptolemy, who had been entrusted with the king's seal, read aloud his Will, but this was not to become effective until Caesar had examined it..."[29] Archelaus' kingship had been announced at the amphitheater in Jericho. The Will had then been read aloud to those assembled. Everyone knew that Caesar must approve the Will before the kingship of Archelaus would be validated. Archelaus himself knew this. This book cannot devote the pages that would be required to go into great detail about the infighting of Herod's family and claims to the throne of Judea. Josephus and other authors have cataloged the animosities and actions in detail. Suffice it to say for now that Archelaus knew there would be serious challenges to his father's last Will. Any delay in his going to Rome to plead his case could result in the loss to himself of the kingdom of Judea.

Recapping events after Herod's death:

> From Josephus: Archelaus spends twenty-five days mourning and traveling from Jericho to Herodium to bury his father. He then travels immediately to Jerusalem. Josephus also tells us that Archelaus was at the temple on Passover.

> From the Bible: Joseph, Mary and Jesus returned from Egypt while Archelaus is reigning. Joseph, Mary and Jesus were in Jerusalem at the temple on Passover.

---

[29] *Josephus with an English Translation*, Ralph Marcus, Phd, p. 461

## Chapter 11

# Another Perspective

Prior to the Passover, Joseph and Mary brought Jesus to the temple in Jerusalem to fulfill a portion of the Law of Moses, the redemption of the first-born. The narrative of Luke describes two important happenings at this event. In chapter two beginning at verse twenty-five, Luke writes, *"Now there was a man in Jerusalem, whose name was Simeon and this man was righteous and devout, looking for the consolation of Israel, and the Holy Spirit was upon him. (V.25) And it had been revealed to him by the Holy Spirit that he should not see death before he had seen the Lord's Christ. (V.26) And inspired by the Spirit he came into the temple; and when the parents brought in the child Jesus, to do for him according to the custom of the law, (V.27)* [redemption of the firstborn] *he took him up in his arms and blessed God and said, (V.28) 'Lord, now lettest thou thy servant depart in peace, according to thy word; (V.29) for mine eyes have seen thy salvation (V.30) which thou has prepared in the presence of all peoples, (V.31) a light for revelation to the Gentiles, and for glory to thy people Israel.' (V.32) And his father and his mother marveled at what was said about him; (V.33) and Simeon blessed them and said to Mary his mother, 'Behold, this child is set for the fall and rising of many in Israel, and for a sign that is spoken against (V.34) (and a sword will pierce through your own soul also), that thoughts out of many hearts may be revealed.' (V.35) And there was a prophetess, Anna, the daughter of Phanuel, of the tribe of Asher; she was of a great age, having lived with her husband seven years from her virginity, (V.36) and as a widow till she was eighty-four. She did not depart from the temple, worshiping with fasting and prayer night and day. (V.37) And coming up at that very hour she gave thanks to God, and spoke of him to all who were looking for the redemption of Jerusalem. (V.38)"* I have quoted verses twenty-five through thirty-eight in full because of the emphasis of the revelation of just who this child, Jesus, was and is. However, the two events depicted here are the recognition of Jesus by Simeon and Anna. Simeon and Anna were both "fixtures" in the temple. Anyone would most likely know who they were and would have questioned the reason for their continual presence. You might be able to imagine the commotion that stirred in the temple area upon these two proclamations.

About one month earlier similar news had been proclaimed in Judea. Shepherds had talked about the birth of a Savior. Multitudes of foreigners had been in Jerusalem asking questions about the birth of a new, "king of the Jews." Now, there were two devout individuals recognized by the priests and people proclaiming once again here He is, "the redemption of Jerusalem", "thy salvation." You would imagine that the hearts of the people would jump with excitement at such news. I believe this was the case. This time though, the Jews did not incite open rebellion upon the proclamation of the redemption of Jerusalem. Archelaus had returned to Jerusalem and was at the temple, available to the questioning of the Jews. Josephus writes that the Jews who gathered at Passover questioned Archelaus. Their question was related to the uprising and demise of the priests Matthais and Judas. They requested that the priest who had been put in place after the deaths of Matthias and Judas, be removed. It had been thirty-two days since their execution and the populace was still in turmoil over their deaths. Questions may have revolved around the reason for Matthias' and Judas' execution and not around the fact that they were executed. The crowd, upon the proclamations by Simeon and Anna, now had full insight into the reason for the execution of the two priests and had once again heard of a new king. In any event though, Archelaus felt threatened, the people became insolent and rebellious and Archelaus had his troops disperse the crowds. In doing so, 3000 worshipers were killed. This massacre at Passover, hastened Archelaus' trip to Rome.

The events at the temple, the uprising initiated by Matthias and Judas and the uprising at Passover are quite remarkable in their timing. It is very interesting that these uprisings as recorded by Josephus, occurred when the Bible states events relevant to Jesus were also taking place. Following on the next page is a graphic timeline indicating the various happenings surrounding the birth of Jesus.

Regardless of the details of the events, the facts are basic. Jesus was born when Herod was king of Judea. Jesus returned from Egypt to Israel after Herod's death, when Archelaus was king.

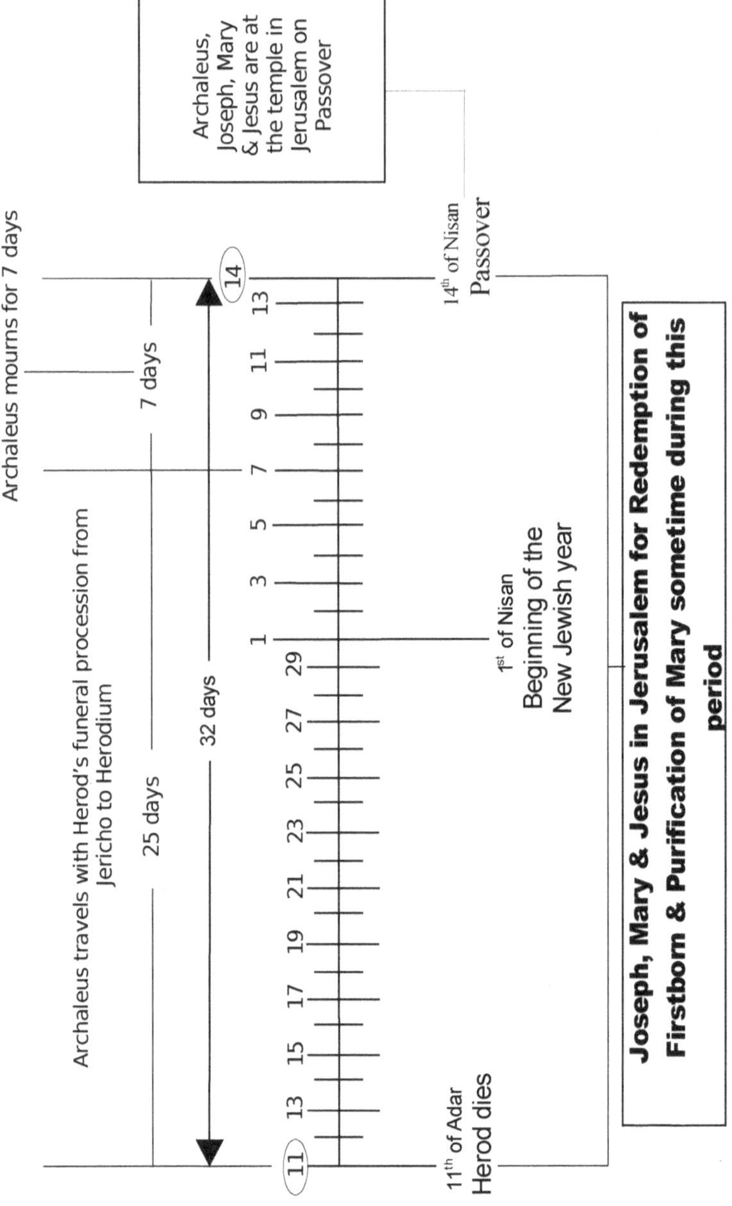
4 B.C.
Archaleus travels with Herod's funeral procession from Jericho to Herodium
Archaleus mourns for 7 days
25 days
7 days
32 days
11 13 15 17 19 21 23 25 27 29
1 3 5 7 9 11 13 14
11th of Adar
Herod dies
1st of Nisan
Beginning of the New Jewish year
14th of Nisan
Passover
Archaleus, Joseph, Mary & Jesus are at the temple in Jerusalem on Passover
Joseph, Mary & Jesus in Jerusalem for Redemption of Firstborn & Purification of Mary sometime during this period

## Chapter 12

# Narrowing the Timeframe

We now know that in order to fit criteria established by history and Levitical requirements, Jesus was born between the eleventh of February (eleventh of Shebat) and the twelfth of March (the tenth of Adar). However, is it possible to narrow the time frame further, possibly even to a specific date? Let us first re-examine some items about the time when Jesus was born.

Jesus was born when Herod was alive. Also, we are told in Matthew chapter two, verse twenty-seven, that the wise men inquired in Jerusalem, *"where is he who has been born king of the Jews?"* This question implies that at the time of the question, the king of the Jews (Jesus) <u>had already</u> been born. We must also remember that after visiting with Joseph and Mary and presenting Jesus with gifts and worshiping Jesus, the wise men were warned in a dream not to return to Herod as Herod had requested. The Bible then in Matthew chapter two, verse sixteen says that Herod became enraged when he found the wise men had tricked him. This verse indicated that Herod expected the wise men to return to him with their report within a reasonable amount of time. And as Bethlehem was only about six miles from Jerusalem, Herod most likely would not have allowed too much time to pass before expecting a report.

The wise men did not return to report to Herod. Judas and Matthias started a rebellion in Jerusalem. Herod died in Jericho on the thirteenth of March (eleventh of Adar). For someone who still might think that a longer span of time may exist concerning

Jesus' birth and remembers mention of an intercalated month called Second Adar, let's see why the year of Jesus'' birth, 4 B.C. did not contain an intercalated month.

Remember on the night Herod died, the eleventh of Adar, there was an eclipse of the moon. An eclipse of the moon can only occur during the time when the moon is in the full moon phase. The full moon occurs half way through the new moon to new moon cycle. As the moon's cycle consists of twenty-nine and one-half days (29-1/2), this means that the full moon occurs at about fourteen days from the time of the full moon to the beginning of the next month.

To help understand the next point about the moon's eclipse, let us change our perspective to the view from the Gregorian calendar. The eleventh of Adar, by direct correlation, equates to the thirteenth of March. Now, we know that the New Year according to the Jewish religious calendar (and the Biblical calendar) occurs the evening before the first new moon after the vernal equinox. The vernal equinox can occur from the twenty-first of March to the twenty-third of March. Therefore, in order for there to be an intercalated month of Second Adar, the addition of fourteen days (from the time of the eclipse during the full moon) would require that the next new moon would occur before the vernal equinox, no later than the twenty-third of March. However, by adding fourteen days to the thirteenth of March we find that the date for the next new moon would occur about the twenty-seventh of March ($13^{th}$ of March + 14 days = $27^{th}$ of March). Since the twenty-seventh of March would be after the occurrence of the vernal equinox, there was not an intercalated month of Second Adar in the year of 4 B.C.

Form previous information we know that the absolute earliest date Jesus could have been born is the eleventh of

February (eleventh of Shebat), sixty-two days before Passover. Additionally, a Levitical requirement generally not considered when studying Jesus' birth, the observance of Passover in Jerusalem, is actually a key element of determining the date of his birth. Joseph, Mary and Jesus were also in Jerusalem at Passover in the year of his birth. Luke chapter two, verse forty-one tells us, *"Now his parents went to Jerusalem every year at the feast of Passover."* Although this verse is contextually associated with the verses following it and not preceding it, the statement is explicit – <u>His parents went to Jerusalem every year at the feast of Passover</u>. This idea is reinforced when again considering that Joseph and Mary had to be and were righteous Jews observing the law of Moses entirely to its letter.

Earlier in our discussions of the Levitical requirements, which were required to be fulfilled, we mentioned the purification of the mother after the birth of a child. Again, Leviticus chapter twelve, verses one through four says, *"The Lord said to Moses, (V.1) 'Say to the people of Israel, If a woman conceives, and bears a male child, then she shall be unclean seven days; as at the time of her menstruation, she shall be unclean (V.2)...Then she shall continue for thirty-three days in the blood of her purifying...(V.4)'"* In order for Mary to have come into the temple and participate in Passover she would have had to completed her days of purification, for according to the twelfth chapter of Leviticus, verse four, a woman could not come into the sanctuary or touch any hallowed thing until the days of her purification were completed. A woman could not even come to the temple to have a priest sacrifice the burnt and sin offerings for purification until the days of purification were completed. Luke chapter two, verse twenty-two tells us specifically that she did go to Jerusalem at the completion of her purification. We are then shown in Luke chapter two, verse twenty-four that Mary had completed her days of purifying and in fulfilling the requirements submitted the proper sacrifices – *"and to offer a sacrifice according the what is said in the law of the Lord, 'a pair of turtledove, or two young pigeons.'"* This rite of purification had to take place forty days after the birth of Jesus. The necessity for purity was so stringent that an alternate observance, Pesah Sheini, was established for those unable to participate in Passover at the required time.[30] So for forty days after the birth of Jesus, Mary could not come into the temple; yet we know she celebrated Passover in Jerusalem in the year of Jesus' birth.

If Mary's completion of purification coincided with the first day of Passover on the fourteenth of Nisan, this would mean that the date Jesus was born is forty days prior to Passover, which was on the fourteenth day of Nisan. Forty days prior to Passover was the third of Adar, eight days before the death of Herod. The third of Adar would be the latest possible date of the purification of Mary. By moving the completion of purification back in time one day at a time and integrating with the requirements of the redemption of the firstborn, we can see that the earliest possible date for Jesus' birth would have been the eleventh of Shebat. The following chart shows this regression of days.

(SEE GRAPHIC ON FOLLOWING PAGE)

---

[30] *A Guide to Jewish Religious Practice*, Isaac Klein, p. 145

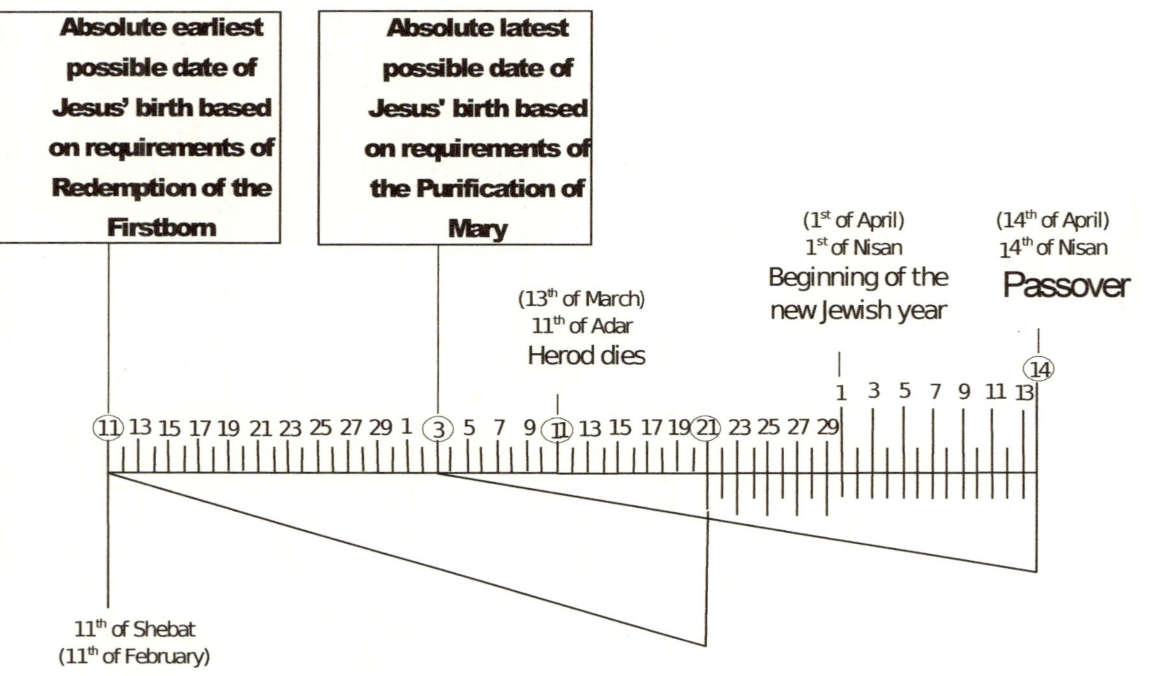
4 B.C.
Absolute earliest possible date of Jesus' birth based on requirements of Redemption of the Firstborn
Absolute latest possible date of Jesus' birth based on requirements of the Purification of Mary
(13th of March)
11th of Adar
Herod dies
(1st of April)
1st of Nisan
Beginning of the new Jewish year
(14th of April)
14th of Nisan
Passover
11 13 15 17 19 21 23 25 27 29 1 3 5 7 9 11 13 15 17 19 21 23 25 27 29
1 3 5 7 9 11 13 14
11th of Shebat
(11th of February)

When incorporating the requirements of the purification of Mary we have now narrowed the time of Jesus' birth to twenty-three possible days. Jesus could only have been born sometime from the eleventh of Shebat to the third of Adar. If we recall, according to the study of the timing of Zechariah's service there were only two times when Jesus could have been born: the end of August or the end of February. The Jewish month of Shebat corresponds to the Gregorian month of February and Adar corresponds to March. The springtime of the year is confirmed as the time when Jesus was born. Now that we have accounted for all the Levitical requirements, can we continue to narrow and define a particular date for his birth?

As we consider the possible date Jesus was born by using criteria established by the purification of Mary we find that the further removed from Passover the date is, the less likely the date would be the actual date of his birth. This is because key events surrounding his birth happened around two specific times: the date of Herod's death and Passover.

Recall that the rebellion led by Judas and Matthais occurred just prior to Herod's death. Also, recall that another rebellion happened at Passover. Sometime between these two events, Simeon and Anna, the prophetess, declared in the temple in Jerusalem the redemption of Jerusalem.

A ten-day span of time exists between the redemption of the firstborn and the purification of Mary. Where was the family of Jesus during these ten days? Verse thirty-nine of the second chapter of Luke tells they remained in Jerusalem, *"And when they had performed everything according to the law of the Lord, they returned into Galilee, to their own city, Nazareth."* Luke chapter two verse forty-one adds even more insight into the time spent in

Jerusalem, *"Now his parents went to Jerusalem every year at the feast of Passover."* Therefore Joseph, Mary and Jesus either remained in Jerusalem for Passover after the rites of the redemption of the firstborn and Mary's purification completed, or returned to Nazareth after the completion of these rites and came to Jerusalem again from Nazareth for the feast of Passover. Verse thirty-nine of Luke chapter two tells us, *"And when they had performed everything according to the law of the Lord, they returned into Galilee, to their own city, Nazareth."* Does this 'everything' include also the celebration of Passover as well as the redemption of the firstborn and rite of purification?

If we evaluate the possibility that Mary's completion of purification occurred prior to the third of Adar, we must consider that the time between Passover and the completion of purification would also be longer. This scenario would require that Joseph, Mary and Jesus would either travel to Jerusalem an extra time or remain in Israel longer. For example, using the previous chart, if Jesus was born ten days earlier than the third of Adar, on the twenty-third of Shebat; then Mary would have completed her purification the fourth of Nisan. Upon completing her purification, Mary Joseph and Jesus would then have remained in Jerusalem an extra ten days (the time between the completion of purification and Passover) or they would have returned to Nazareth only to return again to Jerusalem in ten days in order to observe Passover. Logically, this scenario in not an impossibility however, remaining in Israel for an extended period of time or returning to Nazareth and returning again to Jerusalem would both be contradictory to what the Bible says about the travels of Joseph and Mary and Jesus. The family's journey is explicitly detailed in the Bible.

## Chapter 13

# The Date

Factually, there are only twenty-three possible days when Jesus could have been born. Any specific date chosen within the twenty-three days between the eleventh of February (eleventh of Shebat) and the fifth of March (the third of Adar), 4 B.C. would be based on information not contained within the historical framework. Initially, these twenty-three days were specific enough from my perspective to show when Jesus was born. They also showed that the wise men's visit to Jesus occurred during the first days after his birth. Thus, the question asked at the beginning of the book is answered. However, during the process of researching, additional insight was gained as to a possible specific date for Jesus' birth. As such, I felt I would be remiss not to share this insight with you. Jesus was born the fifth of March (third of Adar) 4 B.C.

One additional fact from the realm of history – earlier, you will recall I stated that the specific day Herod died could be determined. You might say to yourself, "How idiotic, the eleventh of Adar was two thousand years ago and the calendars have been adjusted so.... many times." This indeed might be the case in many instances but remember Herod died on the night of a Jewish fast, the fast of Esther. Interesting? So what, you say, there is still no way to be accurate.

If you study the fast of Esther, you will find that it is observed on the thirteenth of Adar and not the eleventh of Adar. Is this an error in Josephus' accounting of Herod's life? No, the fast of Esther (the fast of Purim) is scheduled to happen on the thirteenth of Adar and Purim begins the fourteenth of Adar. However, as with many Jewish holidays, if the date of the holiday falls on a special day such as the Sabbath, the holiday can be moved according to previously established methods. Purim is a holiday that can be moved. Jewish methods establish that if Purim (the fourteenth of Adar) occurs on a Sunday, then the fast day (the thirteenth of Adar) is observed on the preceding Thursday.[31] As Josephus records that Herod's death was on the eleventh of Adar and states that this was the night of the fast of Esther, then the fast was moved from the thirteenth of Adar to the eleventh of Adar, a Thursday. Herod died on a Thursday. The time now comes to make a transition from the historical facts to theological assertions to explain the reason why Jesus' birth is ascribed to the third of Adar.

---

[31] *A Guide to Jewish Religious Practice*, Isaac Klein, p. 275

## Chapter 14

# Theological Reasoning

Herod died on the eleventh of Adar, a Thursday. Jesus was born on the third of Adar, eight days earlier. By starting on a Thursday and regressing eight days, we can arrive at the day of the week on which the third of Adar fell. Eight days previous to the eleventh of Adar, a Thursday, shows that the third of Adar was a Wednesday. Jesus was born on Wednesday. This day becomes significant when considering other Biblical events that occurred on a Wednesday.

Jesus at the end of his earthly ministry was crucified on a Wednesday. Although traditionally Christians have observed Friday (Good Friday) as the day of his crucifixion, Friday is an impossible day for Jesus' crucifixion and death. Jesus specifically states in Matthew chapter twelve, verse forty that he would be in the earth three days and three nights after his death. This was the case and his resurrection occurred on the first day of the week as is recorded in all four gospels – Matthew, Mark, Luke and John. Sunday is the first day of the week in Jewish chronology, as the seventh day of the week, the Sabbath, is Saturday. Jesus said he would be in the earth, in other words buried, for three days and three nights. In order to meet the requirements of this statement his death would have occurred on the fourth day preceding Sunday. The fourth day preceding Sunday is Wednesday. Jesus was crucified on a Wednesday.

Additionally, there are many Jewish traditions that have in them the wisdom of rabbinical interpretation of the Torah and the prophets. Jewish tradition holds that Adam was created on a Wednesday. Only when we consider the apostle Paul's statements in 1 Corinthians chapter fifteen can a parallel be drawn. Paul in verse twenty-one tells us, *"For as in Adam all die, so also in Christ shall all be made alive."* Paul continues the discussion about resurrection from the dead through chapter fifteen. Then in verse forty-five he makes the statement, *"The first man Adam became a living being; the last Adam became a life-giving spirit."* It is in verse forty-five that Paul associates Jesus with Adam and refers to Jesus as the last Adam - the comparison; the first Adam – the last Adam: hence, the creation of the first Adam on Wednesday and birth of the last Adam on Wednesday. Jesus' birth occurring on Wednesday is reflected in the idea that Jesus was ordained by God from before the foundation of the world to be the last Adam. Ironically, the day of his death is foreshadowed in the day of his birth. Jesus was born on Wednesday.

Jesus was born just before spring began. Spring is a time for new beginnings, as Jesus is a time for new beginnings. The twenty-three possible days when Jesus could have been born occur during the time of the year when one of the four Jewish New Years is celebrated, the New Year of the Tree. The actual "New Year" is celebrated as Tu Bishvat on the fifteenth of the month of Shebat. Although Jesus was born on the third of Adar and the New Year of the Tree is celebrated eighteen days earlier, the significance associated with this celebration is held within the rabbinical interpretations and traditions behind the celebration.

The tradition associated with Tu Bishvat revolves around the idea that Moses' exhortation of the law beginning in Deuteronomy chapter one, verse three, began on the first day of Shebat and ended on the seventh of Adar, with Moses' death.[32]

---

32 *The Jewish Holidays; A Guide & Commentary*, Michael Strassfeld,

This exhortation was second giving of the law; the first was given by God to Moses at Mt. Sinai forty years earlier. The second giving of the law or "Second Sinai" is interpreted that this was Israel's second chance to accept their covenant with God, as they had rejected the first opportunity at Mt. Sinai. In relation, Jesus is seen by many as a second chance to accept God's witness of Himself.

At the center of the second rendering of the law is the idea of the representation of a second Garden of Eden. A reflection also of the opportunity of a second chance. The tradition of the second Garden of Eden continues that in the middle of this period (between the first of Shebat and the seventh of Adar) the Torah stands as the Tree of Eternal Life. As the tree of eternal life stood in the middle of the first Garden of Eden, so also stands the Torah as the Tree of Eternal Life in the middle of the second Garden of Eden. This idea of the Torah standing as the Tree of Eternal Life may be vaguely familiar to you, yet may be entirely alien. Let's expand this as it relates to Jesus.

The Torah as the law of God represents the word of God and as such represents God Himself. The Jewish idea of the Torah standing as the Tree of Eternal Life therefore is not difficult to understand from the Jewish perspective. The idea is not difficult to understand from a Christian perspective either. In John chapter one, verse forty-five, Philip addresses Nathanael and told him, *"We have found him of whom Moses in the law and also the prophets wrote, Jesus of Nazareth, the son of Joseph."* John chapter one, verse one and John chapter one, verse fourteen add further insight into who Jesus is, *"In the beginning was the Word, and the Word was with God, and the Word was God (V.1)...And the Word became flesh and dwelt among us (V.14)..."* However, it

---

p. 184

is not until we hear Jesus' words in John chapter five, verses three and four that we can fully understand the idea of the Torah standing as the Tree of Eternal Life; *"You search the scriptures, because you think that in them you have eternal life; and it is they that bear witness to me; yet you refuse to come to me that you may have life."* Jesus, the one of whom Moses wrote about in the law, the Word of God, the one to whom the scriptures bear witness, the one in whom there is eternal life was born during the time when there exists among the Jews a time of celebration celebrating the Torah standing as the Tree of Eternal Life.

Jesus was born on a Wednesday; at the beginning of spring; during the time when the idea of the Torah standing as the Tree of Eternal Life is celebrated. But, why is the third of Adar such a compelling date?

Jesus in Luke chapter two, verse nineteen while in the temple in Jerusalem and after driving out the money changers, tells a group of Jews, that if the temple would be destroyed, he would rebuild it in three days. Of course, this group of Jews viewed this statement as absurd. The temple in Jerusalem after forty-six years was still under construction. Jesus though was referring to himself as the temple (John chapter two, verse twenty-one).

The temple (Jesus) had been built. Jesus predicted the destruction of the temple and also prophesied of its rebuilding. This rebuilding of the temple was effectuated by the Spirit of God, as told in verse eleven of chapter eight of the book of Romans. The temple was also built by the Spirit of God. If you will recall, in Luke chapter one, verse thirty-five the angel Gabriel tells Mary that her conception would be by the Spirit of God. The construction of the temple began at conception, the temple was destroyed and the temple was rebuilt. When though was the temple completed? If the temple were begun at conception, torn down at Jesus' death and rebuilt at his resurrection, wouldn't it stand to reason that the temple was completed at Jesus' birth?

In the Old Testament of the Bible we read about the historical event of the destruction of the temple in Jerusalem and the destruction of the city of Jerusalem by Nebuchadnezzar, the king of Babylon. The temple that was destroyed by Nebuchadnezzar was known as Solomon's temple and was the first temple constructed in Jerusalem by the Jews. Solomon's temple was a grand structure by all historical references and its elaborateness is described in 2 Chronicles and 2 Kings of the Old Testament.

During this time, the citizenry of Jerusalem and the kingdom of Judah were taken captive to Babylon. These Jews remained in Babylon for seventy years and during those seventy years, Jerusalem and the temple remained in ruins. At the end of seventy years, Cyrus, king of Persia (Babylon was conquered by Persia) made a decree that the Jews should return to Jerusalem to rebuild the temple of God (Ezra chapter one, verses one through three). Among those that returned from Babylon to Jerusalem was the man Zerubbabel the son of Shealtiel.

Zerubbabel and those who went out of Babylon had a very specific task to complete – rebuild the house of God, the temple in Jerusalem. The decree to return to Jerusalem given by Cyrus was given in the first year of his reign. There is no definitive time given when the exiles returned, nor when they arrived in Jerusalem. However, in Ezra chapter three, verse one we are told that in the seventh month, the returned exiles gathered in Jerusalem. At this time they had not begun to rebuild the temple.

After eight months of burnt offerings, the task to rebuild was undertaken. This task began in the second month, in the second year after their return to Jerusalem. It was during this time that the foundation of the temple was laid (Ezra chapter three, verse ten). What a wonderful thing, the house of God was being rebuilt! In fact, Ezra in verses eleven through thirteen of chapter three describes the joy and celebration expressed after the foundation of the temple was laid. But, not everyone was joyful. In verse twelve we find, *"But many of the priests and Levites and heads of fathers' house, old men who had seen the first house, wept with a loud voice when they saw the foundation of the house being laid."* Why were the old men crying when they saw the foundation of the temple being laid?

The foundation of the temple had been laid. The task however was not complete. Zerubbabel and the others attempted to continue their task of rebuilding the temple but adversaries hindered their progress. The contention against rebuilding the temple was so great that Ezra tells us that the hindrances to construction continued through four kings – Cyrus, Ahasuerus, Artaxerxes and Darius.

Cyrus had given the decree to rebuild the temple in the first year of his reign. Zerubbabel and his fellow returned exiles laid the foundation of the temple in the second year of their return to Jerusalem. This event likely occurred during the first years of Cyrus' reign and most probably in the first two years of his reign. Then in the reign of Artaxerxes construction on the temple in Jerusalem ceased entirely. Construction on the temple was not begun again until the second year of the reign of Darius, king of Persia (Ezra chapter four, verse twenty-four). The temple was finished in the sixth year of Darius' reign.

The rebuilding of the temple took some time to finish. According to historical records, Cyrus began his reign in 539 B.C. The reign of Ahasuerus began in 529 B.C. and Darius began his reign in 521 B.C. By this information we can see that even if there is uncertainty as to when the foundation was laid during Cyrus' reign, the time between Ahasuerus' reign and the second year of Darius' reign is ten years. And since the temple was not completed until the sixth year of Darius' reign, the temple took at least sixteen years to complete. In all probability, the construction of the temple took about twenty-four years to complete. The importance regarding the length of time has to with Zerubbabel. At the time the temple had been completed Zerubbabel was no longer mentioned. Verse fourteen of chapter six of Ezra says, *"And the elders of the Jews built and prospered through the prophesying of Haggai, the prophet and Zechariah the son of Iddo..."* Zerubbabel is mentioned continuously throughout the first part of the book of Ezra, yet there appears to be a conspicuous absence of Zerubbabel's name at the time the temple is completed.

The prophesies of Haggai and Zechariah are preserved for our reference as two of the books of the Old Testament of the Bible. When we read the books of Haggai and Zechariah we realize immediately that the oracles of these two prophets of God relate directly to the temple being built by Zerubbabel. Also, we notice that the time of the prophecies are specifically detailed – Haggai's prophecy began, *"In the second year of Darius the king, in the sixth month, on the first day of the month"*; Zechariah's initial prophecy began, *"In the eighth month, in the second year of Darius."* (Haggai chapter one, verse one and Zechariah chapter one, verse one, respectively). The second year of Darius was the year when construction on the temple was resumed after the foundation had been laid several years earlier. In fact, in verses fourteen and fifteen of chapter one of the book of Haggai, Haggai tells us exactly when construction was resumed, *"And the lord stirred up the spirit of Zerubbabel the son of Shealtiel...and they came and worked on the house of the Lord of hosts, their God, (V.14) on the twenty-fourth day of the month, in the sixth month... (V.15)"*

We know by these passages that Zerubbabel was alive when construction of the temple was resumed in the second year of Darius' reign. However, a specific statement in Haggai chapter two is related to a specific statement in chapter four of Zechariah. Zechariah's prophecy, although directed to Zerubbabel at the time when construction on the temple was resumed, is a prophecy of future events related to Jesus. The related statements in Haggai and Zechariah point to the possibility that Zerubbabel was not alive to complete the temple he had begun. This possibility is also addressed in Ezra when Zerubbabel's name isn't mentioned when the temple was completed. Alternately, even if Zerubbabel were alive to see completion of the temple he did not see the promises of God given by the prophet Haggai.

In chapter two, verse three, Haggai is directed by God to speak to Zerubbabel and the remnant which had returned, *"...'Who is left among you that saw this house in it's former glory? How do you see it now? Is it not in your sight as nothing?...'"* Then in chapter two verse nine, Haggai prophesying to Zerubbabel about the temple says, *"The latter splendor of this house shall be greater than the former, says the Lord of hosts; and in this place I will give prosperity, says the Lord of hosts."*

The importance of these two verses is also shown by verse twelve of the third chapter of Ezra, those who had seen the first temple wept when they saw the foundation laid of the second temple. The splendor of the first temple was remembered and this saddened the hearts of those who were now looking at the beginning of the second temple. You see the second temple in no way matched the glory of the first. Literature about the second temple, Zerubbabel's temple, clearly shows that it was extremely inferior in splendor, grandeur and glory to the first temple, Solomon's temple. So, what about God's promise to Zerubbabel that the splendor of the temple would be greater than that of the former?

Not until we look at Zechariah's prophecy concerning the temple can we understand how the splendor of the latter temple would be greater than the splendor of the former. Although Zechariah's prophecies were given at the time construction on Zerubbabel's temple resumed and were given as encouragement to those building the temple, the consensus among theologians is that the prophecies contained in the book of Zechariah are of events future to Zechariah and are directly associated with Jesus. Many Christians are familiar with the phrase, "Not by might, nor by power, but by my Spirit, says the Lord of hosts". This phrase is the last half of verse six of chapter four of Zechariah. The first half of the verse is rarely voiced, yet it is the key to this wonderful familiar phrase, "Not by might, nor by power, but by my Spirit". Zechariah, chapter four begins with a vision seen by Zechariah. The meaning of this vision is then given to Zechariah by an angel in verse six of chapter fours. The first part of verse four says, *"This is the word of the Lord to Zerubbabel."* When we look at the context of the rest of the vision, we can see that the vision refers to the building of the temple. But, what was the word of the Lord to Zerubbabel?

Haggai prophesied to Zerubbabel in the sixth month of the second year of Darius' reign. Zechariah prophesied to Zerubbabel in the eighth month of the second year of Darius' reign. Therefore, Haggai prophesied to Zerubbabel before Zechariah.

The word of the Lord to Zerubbabel was that the glory of the latter temple would be greater than that of the former. Zechariah confirms this word to Zerubbabel, but in a future sense. In doing so, God clearly defines that the building of the temple would be by his Spirit.

The absence of Zerubbabel's name at the time the temple was completed coupled with the fact that the splendor of the second temple was less splendid than Solomon's temple is revealing. Add to these two factors the promise to Zerubbabel and Zechariah's prophecy concerning Jesus and you can begin to see the connection with the time Jesus was born. You see, Jesus refers to himself as the temple and Zerubbabel never saw the glory of the temple as he was promised. In Zechariah chapter four verse seven, we see the last part of the word of the Lord to Zerubbabel – *"...and he shall bring forward the top stone amid shouts of 'Grace, grace to it!'"* In the New Testament, in John chapter one, verse seventeen we find, *"For the law was given through Moses; grace and truth came through Jesus Christ."* The top stone or the "cap stone" is the last stone to be put on. Placing of the top stone signifies completion of construction. In Ezra chapter six, verse fifteen we are told that the temple had been completed, ***"and this house was finished on the third day of the month of Adar..."***

Jesus, the last Adam was born on a Wednesday, was foreshadowed by Adams creation on a Wednesday. Jesus, the Torah standing as the tree of eternal life, is foreshadowed by scriptural interpretation and tradition. Jesus, the temple, is foreshadowed by Zerubbabel's temple.

Jesus was born on the third of Adar, 4 B.C., or by reference to the Gregorian calendar, the fifth of March 4 B.C.! This date may seem astounding and absurd after centuries of tradition of celebrating Jesus' birth on the twenty-fifth of

December. It even clashes with birth dates established as occurring in September of 5 B.C. by various theological interpretations. However, the third of Adar is the only date that accurately reflects all the requirements of logic and historical and religious criteria.

Now that we know when Jesus was born, so what? You say it is interesting information, but what significance does it have.

## Chapter 15

# Reasons to Know

Just as the fact that Jesus did exist as a historical person, gives the non-Christian a foundation to understand Jesus, the facts of the timing of his birth give the Christian a foundation to understand teachings about the ministry of Jesus. Although the entire theological overview of Jesus' ministry will not be addressed here, the information about when Jesus was born allows us to re-examine teachings about the time frame of his ministry, the time frame of his death and the importance of his age as related to prophetical teachings.

Two basic teachings that come into question when adapting this new information are: 1) Jesus was thirty years old when he began his ministry and thirty-three years old when he was crucified, and 2) Calculating prophetic events using the seventy weeks of years in the book of Daniel, chapter nine by using the year of the birth of Jesus to support computations from the decree to rebuild Jerusalem (even for the non-Christian or anyone not familiar with prophecy, the arguments are basic and straight forward).

The first item is the most forthright to address. Conventional teaching that Jesus was thirty years old when he began his ministry is based on verse twenty-three of the third chapter of Luke, *"Jesus, when he began his ministry was about thirty years of age."* This appears fairly straightforward. Jesus was thirty years old. However, verse twenty-three does not say Jesus was thirty when he began his ministry but Jesus was about thirty when he began his ministry. There has been much debate (as in many cases of scriptural interpretation) about the meaning and phrase structure of this verse in original Greek manuscripts. One side of the debate says Jesus was thirty when he began his ministry and the other side says he was about thirty, anywhere from thirty to thirty-five or less than forty years old. How then is this issue of when Jesus began his ministry resolved? Once again the Bible has to be the answer. As with the birth of Jesus, the Bible states quite clearly when Jesus began his ministry.

Prior to Luke telling us that Jesus was about thirty when he began his ministry, Luke gives us a detailed account of when the ministry of John the Baptist began. Luke further defines that John's ministry began before Jesus' ministry. The books of Matthew, Mark and John also confirm that the ministry of John the Baptist began before the ministry of Jesus.

Matthew, chapter three verse one says, *"In those days came John the Baptist, preaching in the wilderness of Judea, 'repent, for the kingdom of heaven is at hand.' For this is he who was spoken of by the prophet Isaiah when he said, "The voice of one crying in the wilderness; Prepare the way of the Lord, make his paths straight.""* Verses four through twelve of Matthew chapter three continue describing John and his ministry. In verse thirteen we then read, *"Then Jesus came from Galilee to the Jordan to John to be baptized by him."* The ministry of John the Baptist began before the ministry of Jesus.

In Mark, chapter one, verse one we find, *"The beginning of the gospel of Jesus Christ, the Son of God. (V.1) As it is written in Isaiah the prophet, 'Behold, I send my messenger before thy face, who shall prepare thy way; (V.2) the voice of one crying in the wilderness: Prepare the way of the Lord, make his paths straight.' (V.3) John the baptizer appeared in the wilderness, preaching a baptism of repentance for the forgiveness of sins... (V.4) – And he preached, saying, 'After me comes one who is mightier than I, the thong of whose sandals I am not worthy to stoop down and untie...(V.7) – In those days Jesus came from Nazareth of Galilee and was baptized by John in the Jordan. (V.9)"* The ministry of John the Baptist began before the ministry of Jesus.

The book of John again shows us the ministry of John the Baptist. Chapter one, verse nineteen begins, "And this is the testimony of John, when the Jews sent priests and Levites from Jerusalem to ask him, *'Who are you?'...(V.19)- He said, 'I am the voice of one crying in the wilderness, 'Make straight the way of the Lord,' as the prophet Isaiah said...(V.23) "... even he who comes after me, the throng of whose sandal I am not worthy to untie"...(V.27) The next day he saw Jesus coming toward him, and said 'Behold the Lamb of God, who takes away the sins of the world;' (V.29) ...'I myself did not know him; but for this I came baptizing with water, that he might be revealed to Israel.' (V.31)"* The ministry of John the Baptist began before the ministry of Jesus.

In each and every book John the Baptist was ministering before Jesus began his ministry. Now that we are fully assured that the ministry of John the Baptist began before the ministry of Jesus, let us see when Luke says the ministry of John the Baptist began.

Luke accounts to us in the beginning of chapter three of the book of Luke exactly when John the Baptist began his ministry. Verse one of chapter three begins, *"In the fifteenth year of the reign of Tiberius Caesar, Pontius Pilate being governor of*

*Judea, and Herod*[33] *being tetrarch of Galilee, and his brother Philip tetrarch of the region of Ituraea and Trachonitus and Lysanias tetrarch of Abilene, (V.1) in the high priesthood of Annas and Caiaphas, the word of God came to John the son of Zechariah in the wilderness; (V.2) and he went into all the region about the Jordan, preaching a baptism of repentance for the forgiveness of sins. (V.3)"* Luke gives some very explicit details about when John the Baptist began his ministry. There is enough evidence to establish more than just a general time. However, since it has been established previously that Luke's statements are accurate, let us only look at one specific item mentioned to show us the time John the Baptist started his ministry.

John began his ministry in the fifteenth year of the reign of Tiberius Caesar. When though, did the reign of Tiberius Caesar begin? Thorough study of Roman history has firmly established that the reign of Tiberius Caesar began in 14 A.D. So, since Tiberius Caesar began his reign in 14 A.D. and John began his ministry in the fifteenth year of Tiberius' reign, John began his ministry in 29 A.D. (14 A.D. + 15 years = 29 A.D.). This seems almost too simple but determining when John's ministry began requires a little basic research and the ability to do simple math. John began his ministry in 29 A.D. Jesus began his ministry after the time John's ministry began. From this information we can determine how old Jesus was when his ministry began.

Earlier, we firmly established that Jesus was born when Herod was alive. We further established that Jesus was born in 4 B.C. By adding the year of Jesus' birth to the year John the Baptist's ministry began, we can arrive at the age of Jesus when he began his ministry; 4 B.C. plus 29 A.D. equals 32 year old

[33] Herod tetrarch of Galilee is the grandson of king Herod (Herod the Great).

[4+29=32 (there is no zero '0' year between B.C. and A.D. determinations)]. Jesus was at least thirty-two years old when he began his ministry. If Jesus began his ministry when he was thirty-two and his ministry lasted for roughly three years, then he would have been at least thirty-five years old when he was crucified. Understanding the basic idea that the Bible is accurate in historical matters shows us quite clearly that Jesus could not have been thirty years old when his ministry began, nor was he crucified at the age of thirty-three.

The second item of teaching, relation of Jesus' birth to chapter nine of the book of Daniel is a little more complicated but, falls along the same lines. The basic idea in chapter nine of the book of Daniel is that there are 490 years related to the occurrence of specific prophetic events. This idea is established in verse twenty-four, *"Seventy weeks of years are decreed concerning your people and your holy city..."* The literal translation of "Seventy weeks of years" is seventy, sevens of years. Thus, seventy, sevens of years is calculated as: 70 x 7 = 490 years. The prophetic events described throughout chapter nine are commenced at a point in time related in verse twenty-five, *"Know therefore and understand that from the going forth of the word to restore and build Jerusalem..."*

In order to completely understand the timing of events let us back up and take a look at when Daniel saw the vision from which the prophecy emanates and what the condition of Jerusalem was at the time of the vision. Daniel was in Babylon during the first year of Darius, son of Ahasuerus, king of the Chaldeans. About sixty-five years prior to the prophesy Jerusalem had been besieged by Nebuchadnezzar and had been laid waste. The temple of the Jews in Jerusalem had been torn down, and the hallowed articles of worship had been taken to Babylon. Furthermore, the walls of Jerusalem had been totally destroyed, the inhabitants of the city (of which Daniel was one) had been taken to Babylon and essentially Jerusalem was uninhabited.

Now, since we understand that Jerusalem was a destroyed city at the time of the vision, the importance of the statement, "Know therefore and understand that from the going forth of the word to rebuild and restore Jerusalem" becomes evident. Daniel has this vision after the dispersion to Babylon in 586 B.C. and before the return of the exiles from Babylon in 516 B.C. The significance of the vision results in that according to historians, the word to restore Jerusalem was given by Artaxerxes in 458 B.C. or 457 B.C.

The vision of Daniel described in chapter nine of the book of Daniel is traditionally interpreted that from the going forth of the word to restore and rebuild Jerusalem to the coming of the anointed one there would be sixty-nine weeks of years, or 483 years (69 x 7 = 483). There are two approaches of determining the anointed one using this information.

One approach of interpreters is, by taking the year that the word to restore Jerusalem was given and adding to it the number of years for the coming of the anointed one, a specific year can be attributed to the vision. This attributed year would also confirm who the referenced anointed one is. Following this method of calculation it can be determined that the specific year attributed to the vision is either 25 A.D. or 26 A.D. (458 B.C. + 483 years = 25 A.D.; 457 B.C. + 483 years = 26 A.D.).  Although the years of 25 A.D. and 26 A.D. hold no significance from a Biblical or non-Biblical perspective, Jesus is the person attributed as the person described as the anointed one. To verify this perspective interpreters take the date of the end of 483 years and subtract from it thirty years, because Jesus was about thirty when his ministry began. As you can see, this method already presumes whom the anointed one is. Jesus' birth is thereby calculated as occurring in 4 B.C. (when using 26 A.D.) or 5 B.C. (when using 25 A.D.).

The other approach uses the same numbers and dates, (483 years added to 458 B.C.) to arrive at a resulting date of 30 A.D. or 33 A.D. The vision of Daniel from this perspective is interpreted as representing the time of the end of Jesus' earthly ministry. When this method is used dates must be "fudged" to move the resulting date to 30 A.D. or 33 A.D. For example, many times interpreters say the decree to restore Jerusalem was <u>about</u> 450 B.C. (not 458 B.C.) and with the addition of 483 years the resulting date conveniently becomes 33 A.D.

The calculations are indeed intriguing. Although data that establishes dates in history can allow the dates to variable by several years, God is not variable. God has shown He is very specific and accurate when He gives us dates to reference. As shown earlier, Jesus was not thirty when he began his ministry nor was he thirty-three when he was crucified. These calculations based upon chapter nine of the book of Daniel therefore become just manipulation of numbers to support an interpretative perspective and are totally contrary to the basic facts of Jesus' birth as set out in the Bible.

Although, only two traditional teachings have been highlighted, there are also many other theological and prophetical significant dates and events associated and calculated from the key point in history, the birth of Jesus. This date is specifically, literally established in the Bible. We must remember that there are three very basic fundamental points to remember when determining the date of Jesus' birth; 1) Jesus was born when

Herod was alive; 2) Joseph, Mary and Jesus returned out of Egypt when Herod was dead; 3) The laws of Moses had to be fulfilled even in Jesus' infancy.

## Chapter 16

# Consider

I urge you to read other writings about when Jesus of Nazareth was born. In most cases the birth of Jesus is hinged upon whether Quirinius was governor of Syria prior to 6 A.D. This issue, is of course, relevant to Jesus' birth. However, the time of Quirinius' governorship of Syria is just one element in Luke's chronological perspective of when Jesus was born. The additional elements of Luke's narrative states that, "the whole world was enrolled" and that, "this was the first enrollment." These are elements that are not to be dealt with separately, but are in fact a part of the entire chronology. Quirinius' governorship of Syria, the enrollment of the entire world and the statement that this enrollment was the first enrollment taken together, direct us to one specific point in time. Also, Luke's chronological perspective is only one narrative that directs us to when Jesus of Nazareth was born.

Again, the basic fundamental to remember when considering when Jesus of Nazareth was born is: <u>Jesus was born when Herod the Great, king of Judea, was alive</u>. This is a point that I have never seen argued in the negative. As this chronological perspective by Matthew is unarguably accepted, why is the accuracy of Luke's chronological perspective denied? For, the time of Herod's death has also been unarguably accepted as occurring on the thirteenth of March 4 B.C. This fact alone bears witness that Jesus' birth could not have occurred after the thirteenth of March 4 B.C. It is interesting to reflect on Herod's death. The date of his death has been known and written about for centuries. The date of the occurrence of Herod's death is not a fact "revealed" by modern scholarship. Yet, the correlation between his death and Jesus' birth seems to have eluded most everyone.

The birth basics as to the time of Jesus' birth are just "basic". Which again brings us back to 2 Timothy chapter three, verse sixteen, *"All scripture is inspired by God and profitable for teaching, for reproof, for correction and for training in righteousness."* Jesus was born at a very unique time in history. He was born around the time a king dies, whose time of death was verified by an astronomical event. He was also born when the culture of which he was a part of had very strict requirements as to the time of and geographical locations for specific religious observances. Also, we find that there were many recorded historical events that occurred which are very specific about detailing the time of his birth. Consider, if we cannot trust what the Bible says about the elemental things, such as the birth of Jesus; how can we trust what it has to say about the deeper things of God, such as the promise of eternal salvation by confessing with your lips that Jesus is Lord and believing in your heart that God raised him from the dead?

## Alphabetical Index

# Bibliography

*The Old and the New Testament of the Holy Bible Revised Standard Version*, Toronto, New York, London, Thomas Nelson & Sons, 1952

*Talmudic and Rabbinical Chronology*, Edgar Frank, Jerusalem, Israel, Philip Feldheim Inc., Feldheim Publishing Ltd., 1956 reprinted 1977

*The Legacy of Egypt*, edited by S.R.K. Glanville, London, Oxford at the Claredon Press, 1942, 43, 47, 53, 57

*In the Provinces of the Roman Empire from Caesar to Diocletian*, Theodore Mommsen, translated by William P. Dickson, D.D., LL.D., New York, Charles Scribener's Sons, 1887

*The Augustan Principate in Theory and Practice during the Julio-Claudian Period*, Mason Hammond, New York, Russell & Russell, 1968

*The History of Human Society – The Romans 850 B.C.-A.D. 337*, Donald R. Dudley, edited by J. H. Plumb, New York, Alfred A. Knopf, Inc., 1970

*Rome the Augustan Age; A Source Book*, Part 1 edited by Kitty Chisholm and John Ferguson, Part 2 edited by Kitty Chisholm, London, New York, Oxford University Press, 1987

*Josephus; Vol. 9, p. 2; English Translation*, Louis H. Feldman, Associate Professor of Classics, Yeshiva University, Cambridge, Mass., Harvard University Press, 1965

*Syria a Short History: Being a Condensation of the Author's 'History of Syria including Lebanon and Palestine'*, Phillip K. Hitti, Professor Emeritus of Sematic Literature on the William and Annies S. Paton Foundation Princeton University, New York, The McMillian Company, 1959

*The Province of the Roman Empire from Caesar to Diocletian*; Translated with the Author's Santion and Additions by William P. Kickson D.D., LL.D., Theodore Mommsen, New York, Charles Scribner's Sons, 1887

*Rabbinical Mathematics and Astronomy*, W. M. Feldman, New York, Hermon Press, 1965

*Becoming a Jew*, Maurice Lamm, Middle Village, NY, Jonathon David Publishers, 1991

*The Code of Maimonides; Book Eight the Book of Temple Service*, translated from the Hebrew by Mendell Levittes, M.A., New Haven, Yale University Press, 1957

*Josephus with an English Translation*, Ralph Marcus, Phd., Late Professor of Hellenistic Culture in the University of Chicago, completed and edited by Allen Wilkgren, Phd., Cambridge, Mass., Harvard University Press, 1963

*A Guide to Jewish Religious Practice*, Isaac Klein, Volume VI in the Moreshet Series, Studies in Jewish History, Literature and Thought, New York, The Jewish Theological Seminary of America, 1979

*The Star of Bethlehem An Astronomer's Confirmation*, David Huges, Walker & Company, New York, 1979

*The Jewish Holidays, A Guide & Commentary*, Michael Strassfeld, New York, Harper & Row Publishers, 1985

www.ingramcontent.com/pod-product-compliance
Lightning Source LLC
LaVergne TN
LVHW090614110826
845146LV00001B/379

* 9 7 9 8 9 9 8 8 5 4 6 1 3 *